OUR ONLY HOPE
Living a Life of Freedom

Grace Rockwell

WESTBOW
PRESS®
A DIVISION OF THOMAS NELSON
& ZONDERVAN

This book is a work of non-fiction. Unless otherwise noted, the author and the publisher make no explicit guarantees as to the accuracy of the information contained in this book and in some cases, names of people and places have been altered to protect their privacy.

WestBow Press books may be ordered through booksellers or by contacting:

WestBow Press
A Division of Thomas Nelson & Zondervan
1663 Liberty Drive
Bloomington, IN 47403
www.westbowpress.com
844-714-3454

www.GraceRockwell.com
Email: Grace@GraceRockwell.com
Blog: gracerockwell.wordpress.com
Facebook: Grace Rockwell, Author
IG: gracerockwell68
Twitter: @GraceRockwell68
Goodreads: Grace Rockwell

All Scripture quotations are taken from THE HOLY BIBLE, NEW INTERNATIONAL VERSION®, NIV® Copyright © 1973, 1978, 1984 by Biblica, Inc.™ Used by permission. All rights reserved worldwide. Words in parentheses added by the author.

Printed in the United States of America

ISBN: 978-1-6642-0540-6 (sc)
ISBN: 978-1-6642-0539-0 (hc)
ISBN: 978-1-6642-0541-3 (e)

Library of Congress Control Number: 2020917593

Print information available on the last page.

WestBow Press rev. date: 10/20/2020

I dedicate this book to the six ladies who never stopped praying for me.

CONTENTS

INTRODUCTION

And I will fear no evil
For my God is with me
Oh no, You never let go
Through the calm and through the storm
Oh no, You never let go
In every high and every low
Still I will praise You, still I will praise You
—*You Never Let Go* by Matt Redman

Do you ever get a song stuck in your head? It might be a jingle from some commercial that plays a thousand times each night during your favorite show. Or maybe it's a catchy tune from the radio. Then again it might be the song lyrics that get stuck on repeat. Most of the time, the songs that get stuck in my head are very uplifting, positive songs. (But come on! They are often on repeat for days or weeks at a time. Enough already!) As I am writing this now, I've had the song *You Never Let Go* by Matt Redman stuck in my head for weeks. I've listened to other songs in the meantime, but it just won't go away. Ugh! At this point I'm like, "OK. Must be I'm supposed to really think about the lyrics and the overall meaning of the song." I've come to the conclusion that this song is really a reflection of my life, and all I have been through over the years.

Speaking of my life, I've been looking back over the past fifty years and am feeling like now is the right time to share my story. I've also been praying a lot about where I've been, where I am, and where I want to be. Prayers about what the next fifty years will bring. Prayers about how to share my story.

Last night as I was going to sleep, I felt the power and gravity of who God is. It was storming with a lot of lightening and loud thunder. The rain was pouring down on the house and I thought, "Wow, God! There really is NO stopping You!" Then I went to sleep praying, "Lord, I don't know when you want me to share my story, or even if I'm supposed to write my story. But if it is Your will, please give me the words. I can't do this on my own. I need some direction here. Thank You, Father. Amen."

The next thing I know my alarm is going off. It was time to get up and get ready for my morning appointment. The problem was that I didn't want to wake up. I was too involved in my dream and I needed to know how it ended. Instead of going back into the dream, I felt the need to start writing down everything I could remember from the dream. You see, a few weeks ago I read a book by Jane Hamon called *Dreams & Visions*. Jane is a Christian teacher who really changed my opinion about dreams through her book. I will never again think of my dreams as silly, passing whims of the subconscious mind. Instead, I now pay more attention and try to really think through my dreams and what they might mean. Jane states that, "individuals should examine their own dreams and learn to listen to God's Holy Spirit through this God-ordained method of communication." (19) She goes on to explain that it is important to write down what we can remember upon waking. This is because it is only in those fleeting moments that we can remember. Jane recommends keeping paper and pen beside your bed so you can write before you even get out of bed in the morning. Or if you wake in the middle of the night.

So that's exactly what I did. I wrote, and I wrote, and I wrote. Nine sticky notes later, I had jotted down all of the elements I could remember. And as I wrote, I realized that God was answering my prayer from the previous night. He was giving me some of the ideas for this book. Part of my life story is within each element and character throughout my dream:

> Protagonist - Little Girl
> Antagonists - The Enemy, Young Mama, Old Mama
> Supporting Character - The Caregiver

My dream started inside a church. The young mama had brought her little girl to the church looking for answers. The little girl had been telling her things that did not make sense. She was telling her mama about things she could do, but the mama knew those things were not possible. Mama had realized that her daughter would only make these claims while she was taking her pain medication. At the church was the little girl's caregiver. The caregiver tried to tell the mama that her daughter's allegations were true. But it wasn't the medication causing the phenomena.

The little girl claimed that she could see and do things that seemed impossible. Sometimes she would look in a mirror and not see her reflection. Her caregiver had actually seen some of these things herself, but was unable to convince the young mama of the truth.

As the two ladies were conversing, the caregiver tried to explain that the little girl had been thinking like an adult from a very young age. She said, "Your daughter knows what you mean when you tell her that 'Raspberry Rose' is coming to visit. She knows that means your time of the month." The little girl was so upset that her mama didn't believe her or the caregiver. The girl was scared of her mama and didn't want to upset her. Her mama was pregnant at the time they were at the church. But the little girl knew that the baby in her mama's belly had gone to Heaven. She was scared to tell anyone about the baby for fear of getting into trouble and making things worse. The trip to the church was fruitless. The young mama still didn't believe her daughter's allegations, or the words from the caregiver.

The next scene opens into a small apartment. There are two beds with a TV between them. The young mama is sleeping in one bed, and the old mama is sleeping in the other bed. The unborn baby is in the corner sleeping in a beautiful, white lace bassinet. The apartment and its furnishings are old, dusty, and falling apart. The little girl enters the apartment and starts using her powers to regenerate everything in sight. She starts in the bathroom and with her simple words, she speaks into existence a new sink, a new bathtub, new towels, new paint on the walls, and new flooring. She then proceeds to the large room with the two beds, TV and bassinet. She starts to regenerate the walls, the decor—but then the enemy comes on the TV and starts telling the little girl lies. Lies that she "can't do this." "She is not good enough." "She should give up." As the enemy speaks, she starts to feel horrible and her powers begin to fade. Then her body morphs into a black cat. As the enemy continues to fill the room with lies, her cat body starts to fall apart. Limbs fall off and fur falls to the floor.

Enter the caregiver. The caregiver walks over to the TV and switches it off. She then starts praying over the little girl. She pleads with God to put the little girl back together. As she prays, the girl regains her body parts and starts turning back into a child. The caregiver continues to fervently pray over her until the girl is back to normal. But when the caregiver stopped praying, the little girl would start falling apart again. After several times of this happening, the caregiver realizes that she must fervently pray without ceasing over this precious little girl.

Once the girl is back to being completely normal, she continues her mission to regenerate the apartment. She is able to speak into existence fresh, clean walls, decor, linens, and she even cleans up the antique furniture that was falling apart. The little girl spoke new life into that apartment, and the caregiver never stopped praying for her.

After some deep soul searching, I was able to interpret my dream as huge parts of my life so far. The little girl is me. The enemy is Satan, and the mama (young and old) is my biological mom. The caregiver is a representation of six godly women who have loved on and prayed for me throughout my life. And finally, the baby represents the unborn babies who my mom had miscarried before my brother and I were born.

PART I

My Story

ONE

The Beginning

For God so loved the world that he gave his
one and only Son, that whoever believes in him
shall not perish but have eternal life.
—John 3:16

It was the 1960s, and my parents had already been married
for several years. Dad had served time in the army, and they
were now settling into a typical, middle-class community in
the Midwest. They both had good jobs working full-time. Mom
had been pregnant a few times but kept having miscarriages.
In the spring of 1964, Mom was so happy to finally be bringing
home a baby boy. My brother, Luke, made a family of three,
and he was the apple of her eye. My mom often told the story
of my brother's birth and how she had asked her doctor if
she might be able to get pregnant again. The doctor had told

her a resounding, "No. Not with all of the complications you have had."

At that point Mom decided to continue with her career and work her way up the corporate ladder. But then in 1968 came the hiccup in her plan. I was born on a cold November Sunday; and then there were four. After I was born, Dad knew it was time for a bigger house. My parents bought a piece of land and built a large three-bedroom house with a beautiful pond full of fish and lots of room for a garden. I was two years old when we moved into the house, and Luke was six.

To say that our family was not close is an understatement. There was not a loving relationship among any of us really, and our house lacked affection and love. Luke was always off fishing, playing sports, or hanging out with the neighbor boys. Dad could always be found in his garden or his workshop when he was at home. Mom was the socialite of the family. When not at work, she would be at the bowling alley, a church meeting, or shopping with a friend. I, on the other hand, was home all the time. I was the only reader in my family and would often be curled up with my books or writing stories. Or playing with my dolls. My dolls were my companions when nobody else was around. They were loyal, and I was always a very good mother to them.

Within the first couple years of my life, my parents knew there was something extremely wrong with me. I would cry and cry for no apparent reason and would often vomit. At the age of two I had my tonsils removed in hopes that would help me feel better. It did not. It wasn't until the age of five, when I could say "my head hurts" that my doctor figured out what was wrong. He diagnosed me with Migraine. From that point on, just like in my dream, Mom went looking for answers. There were so many questions: Why does she have migraines? How do we make them stop? How can we prevent them? And like my dream, the search was fruitless.

Because of the migraines, I spent a lot of time in bed or playing quietly in my room. I was a very lonely child who just wanted someone to be tender toward me and to love on me. My love languages are physical touch and words of affirmation. But I got none of that at my house as a child. I was six weeks old when Mom went back to work full-time, and I started going to daycare. My daycare provider (one of the six caregivers in my dream) has told me how I would lay in the crib and cry all day long. And as a toddler, I would go sit in a corner and cry all day. She nor any of the other children were able to console me. It was only when Mom showed up at the end of the day that I would stop crying. My theory is that I was yearning for the affection and love of my mom. I now look back on photos of me as a baby, and in all of them I am alone. There is not one photo showing either parent holding me, playing with me, or caring for me. I remember one time when Mom was looking for something in her cedar chest and came across my baby book. It was still in the box, and there was nothing in it. Nothing written down, no photos, no lock of hair. It was as if I had never been born. Just like the lack of a reflection in the mirror of my dream, it was as if I didn't exist. I still have that baby book today, and it is still empty.

Instead of a loving marriage, my parents argued and yelled at each other all of the time. They never agreed on anything. Dad was soft-spoken, and he always let Mom do all of the talking. He had also given in to let her rule the household. Whatever she wanted was the way it was going to be. The fighting really got to Dad, and he would spend every Friday night with the guys at the local lodge to decompress. I remember one Friday night when he came home from the lodge, and they started fighting.

It scared me so much that I ran to my neighbor's house crying. Their house was a safe place.

Mom would yell at me too. It was as if I could do nothing right and everything was my fault. I don't think my brother ever got into trouble. He was Mom's favorite—and still is, fifty years later. Mom would slap me in the face when I spoke out of turn. I think her idea was that children should be seen and not heard. I had no voice in our family, and Mom has never listened to anything I say.

Our next door neighbors, the Brown's, were amazing. They never yelled or argued whatsoever. Not in front of us kids anyway. They loved on each another, their three children, and me. The mom, Jennifer, is another one of the caregivers from my dream. She was a stay-at-home mom who would take care of me when I was sick during the day. Her two daughters were about my same age. Jennifer has told me about the first time she met me and my mom. I was four, her oldest daughter was two, and they had just moved in next door. While our moms talked, us girls went into my room to play. But before long, I came out to the living room crying and all upset because her daughter had made a mess with my toys and would not put them away. Jennifer was taken aback by my four-year-old breakdown and how my thinking was far beyond my years. Sound familiar? The caregiver in my dream said that my thinking was like that of an adult.

Starting school at the age of five brought a whole new set of problems. The school would call Mom at her work each time I got sick. I remember spending many hours in the principal's office with his trash can next to me, for when I needed to vomit. Mom never seemed to rush getting to the school, even though she only worked about three minutes from there. Once she arrived, we would take the very long thirty minute drive to the doctor's office. It was almost unbearable being in the car that long on a sunny day. The car was warm and made me more sick to my stomach, and the bright sun hurt my eyes, making the headache even more painful. The doctor would give me an injection of pain medication and send us on our way. We would get back in the car for the excruciating return trip. Mom would drop me off at Jennifer's house and go back to work. I asked Jennifer about this recently, and she said, "Your mom would bring you to my house and have you go to sleep on my living room carpet in a sleeping bag. We always put a pan beside you in case you threw up. Then your mom would go back to work. It was so sad." This scene played out all of the time over my thirteen grade school years.

I was always a good student, trying my best to get good grades. Elementary school was no exception. I loved school, but having two perfectionistic parents didn't help. I felt like I had to do everything right or I'd get in trouble. Sometimes my grades would suffer due to so many missed sick days. When I was in sixth grade, I barely passed by the end of the school year. My teacher and parents decided to give me the option of a do-over. If I wanted to repeat the grade, it would help me catch up with all I had missed that first year. A second chance? Really? Wow, was I excited! That was the only time Mom has ever given me a second chance for anything. I was determined to do better the second time around and maybe even make her proud of me. My second year in sixth grade was much better, academically. But it also brought another health concern. I was diagnosed with hyperthyroidism and was scheduled for surgery. My surgeon removed half of my thyroid, and we all had hopes that it would cure the migraines. It did not.

I always thought the Brown family was amazing because they were loving toward one another and their home was peaceful. I wished that I could live with them. I didn't know what they had, but I wanted it. They were a God-fearing family, but so was ours. Both of our families went to church on Sundays, and we both had Bibles in our homes. One summer when I was eleven years old, Jennifer invited me to go with her and the girls to Vacation Bible School at their church. School in the summer? Cool! I was in.

Learning has always been a passion of mine. And learning a new Bible verse each day was fun. But the most important thing that summer was what I learned about Jesus. I learned that God loved me so much that He sent His only son, Jesus, to Earth to die on a cross for my sins. God loved me so much. Wow! This was a new concept to me. I also learned that if I were to believe in Jesus and ask Him into my heart, I would go to heaven instead of hell when I died. Because God loved me so much, I could go to heaven! I was overwhelmed by this truth because it was a love like I had never known before.

It didn't all make sense to me, but that summer in 1980 I was given a second chance. A second chance to be born again. I was in tears. Tears of joy filled my eyes as I went forward that morning to ask Jesus into my heart. From then on I've always had the complete assurance that God loves me. That day changed everything!

I learned that church was a place to learn about God, not to just pass the time playing games and gathering with friends. It seemed strange to me that I had never learned these things at my church. I wanted a Bible so I could learn more on my own, and in September, I got one. My first Bible was a Revised Standard Version with red letters and beautiful artwork throughout. I thought it was cool how Jesus's words were all in red. And so began my spiritual journey.

TWO

Adolescence

When the night has been too lonely
And the road has been too long
And you think that love is only
for the lucky and the strong
Just remember in the winter
Far beneath the bitter snow lies the seed
That with the sun's love, in the spring
Becomes the rose

—*The Rose* by Bette Midler

I'm fairly good at discerning a positive versus a negative atmosphere. I knew my house did not have a good atmosphere. Yet the Brown's house was very good. Have you heard of the experiments done by Dr. Emoto in regards to the impact of positive and negative words? Japanese scientist, Masaru Emoto, made a series of tests and discovered some very interesting results. He realized that both positive and negative words can have an influence on water's structure by changing water's crystals. During his study of water, Emoto came to some fascinating conclusions. He came to a belief that our emotional energy and words can change the physical structure of water. Emoto's tests mostly consisted of putting water in glasses and then exposing them to different words, pictures, and music. Then he froze the water and analyzed how the ice crystals looked under a microscope. Through his research and analysis, he came to the conclusion that if we "influence" water with positive words, pictures, or music; the ice crystals will be nicely formed. On the other hand, if one puts water near negative influences, such as saying negative words, or if you turn on some loud heavy metal music, the results will be the total opposite. Those crystals will be distorted and formed in an ugly and negative formation. You can google Dr. Emoto and find photos of the crystals. The nicely formed crystals are beautiful and look like snowflakes. The ugly ones look like brown nasty mud.

Dr. Emoto also did the experiment using rice in three glasses of water. He discovered that over a month's time, the glass given positive words and energy started to ferment and give off a pleasant aroma. The rice stayed white throughout this time. On the other hand, the rice given negative words and energy turned black. And the one he ignored began to rot. The Dr. believes that the most important impact is on children. He has stated that, "We should take care of them (children), give them attention, converse with them. And indifference does the greatest harm."

There is no doubt in my mind that the negative words and

energy were at work in my home growing up. There was so much indifference and negativity as opposed to the positive, loving words and energy at the house next door. Not only was I lonely and in pain as a child, but I was often plagued with depression. The depression has always been an after effect of the migraine attacks.

Another thing that added to the negative atmosphere was the behavior of my mom. Like I said, my brother was rarely at home, and at the age of thirteen he got his first job at the local sporting goods store. He would ride his moped back and forth to work after school. And when he turned sixteen, he got his first car and would drive to work. One day soon after getting his driver's license, Luke was at work when he got the phone call. It was the sheriff's department. He was asked to come down to the jail and pick up our mom because she had been arrested for shoplifting. I was twelve at the time and will never forget that day. He drove into our driveway to drop mom off and then sped back out. I believe it was my dad who told me what had happened. I was in shock. But it was quickly swept under the rug and never mentioned again. Mom ended up losing her job at the bank and started looking for employment out of town. Funny thing is that Mom always acted as though nothing happened. As you can imagine, my brother and I lost respect for her that day. Neither one of us has ever trusted her since. Unfortunately, still to this day, she doesn't believe she did anything wrong. Ever.

One time I learned that Mom was banned from a local nursing home. She had been caught stealing money from one of the elderly residents. Of course she denied that too. It has always been that what she says is the truth and she can do no wrong.

I, on the other hand, couldn't seem to do anything right. I

was growing up and figuring things out. My anger started to build; Mom and I butted heads often, and my rebellion started in. I had realized that Mom usually didn't believe anything I told her (like in my dream), so I started telling her lies. I figured she wouldn't believe me anyway, so it was no big deal. I would lie to her about where I was and what I was doing.

At the age of fifteen, I was a high school freshman and started dating my first boyfriend. I was head over heels in love. What girl wouldn't be smitten by a handsome boy who doted on her? Bob quickly became my everything. He was so kind and loving toward me. He listened to me, wrote poems for me, and we had so much fun together. He also gave me the physical affection I had desperately needed for the first fifteen years of my life. He gave me attention when I was sick too. He hated seeing me in pain so often. I was sixteen when something I don't remember happened, and Mom forbid me to see him anymore. She never has liked him and has never been afraid to tell me so. But she couldn't stop me from seeing him at school. One day at school a girlfriend of mine had a bad asthma attack. She needed someone to ride home with her to make sure she was ok. I was happy to go and made the trip out to her house which was about fifteen minutes from town. She lived out near Bob's house, and we made the plan that he would drive me home that evening. But Mom was not happy about that.

When I called to tell her what had happened and that Bob would bring me home, she screamed into the phone and told me to get home now! She was so mad that I was instantly afraid of her and did not want to go home. After talking with Bob and his mom, Mercy, we decided that she (Mercy) would take me home and explain everything to my mom. But when we arrived, Mom wouldn't even let Mercy talk. Mom was very rude and nasty to her, telling her that her son was to have nothing to do with me anymore. I was bawling and telling Mercy that Mom just did not understand. I really did not want Mercy to leave me there with Mom. I just ran to my room and locked myself in for the rest of the night.

By this stage in my life, the migraines had gotten worse. Going to the doctor's office for an injection was no longer working. And the various doctors and treatments we had tried all failed. The only alternative was to go to the hospital for more aggressive treatment. By the time I was a teenager, everyone in the emergency room knew me by name. On a few occasions when Mom did not take me to the hospital right away, I ended up dehydrated from so much vomiting. I would then be admitted and given IV fluids with pain medication for a couple of days.

One morning when I was sixteen, I was in so much pain I could not get out of bed to go to school. Mom and Dad went to work, and I stayed in bed all day trying to sleep it off. When Mom got home, she just let me sleep thinking that was what I needed. I still hadn't woke up the next day when she left for work. This happened two or three days in a row. When she finally did wake me up, I was extremely dehydrated and unable to open my left eye. Back to the hospital we went, and I was admitted. An eye specialist came in and determined that the third nerve in my left eye was paralyzed. I was unable to open my eye, or look to the left, or look up. I was scared to say the least, thinking I may never see again out of that eye. The doctor assured me that the nerve would restore itself, but it would take some time. He gave me a black eye patch to wear until it healed. It was awful! I was a sixteen year old girl having to wear that ugly black patch to school for a week.

After that hospital stay and my eye healed, I felt like I had been beaten down by one horrifying migraine after another. I sat down with pencil and paper and here is what I wrote:

The Storm

The sky is clear and all is well, or so it seems.
Suddenly, without warning, a giant
bolt of lightening—it all begins: The Storm.
Inside the tiny, fragile world The
Storm rages. But why this Storm with so much
destruction?! This world is as well
as it could possibly be. The Storm messes
things up so badly. During The Storm
everything is out of perspective. It is so
painful! Even with such modern
technology, no one can figure out The Storm. That streak
of lightening is there—constantly. Drugs—many drugs
have been tested to rid The Storm—no luck! Just
messes up the world even more. The after-
effects are even worse. It takes so long
to get the world back to normal. But will it
ever be normal again?! Sure—all is
healed, but what about the next time The
Storm hits? Then what? Will the world
heal then? The world was becoming so beautiful,
but after The Storm—just barely average.

It was the Thanksgiving weekend after my seventeenth birthday. Bob and I were back together and attending my church on Sunday morning. Mom had given up trying to keep us apart. We had a new pastor at the time, and for the first time at my church, I heard the salvation message. I knew at the time I had been living in sin and it was time to get right with God. I went forward that morning and told the pastor I wanted to rededicate my life to the Lord. And I did. It was about a week later when it was confirmed that I was pregnant. I wasn't proud of it but was excited to have a family of my own. Bob and I knew we would get married and have a family someday. It just happened sooner than later. And I was more than happy to move out of Mom and Dad's house.

The hardest part was telling our parents about the pregnancy. I was scared stiff to tell my mom. Of course, she blew up at us. But Dad, on the other hand, told her to sit down and be quiet. (The one and only time I saw my dad stand up to her.) He was happy for us. And I think he really understood how I felt about Bob. Since we were both under the age of 18, we had to have our parents sign for us to get a marriage license. Mom refused. But Dad was happy to do it. Telling Bob's parents (Brett and Mercy) was completely different. Although they were disappointed in us, they still loved on us and graciously allowed me to come live with them at the farm after Bob and I got married. They would become my second set of parents who really raised me the rest of the way. (And Mercy was one of the caretakers that I mentioned in my dream.) In January 1986 Bob and I were married in his church by his pastor, Pastor Bowman.

THREE

Marriage and Babies

Be strong and courageous... Be strong and very courageous. Be careful to obey all the law my servant Moses gave you; do not turn from it to the right or to the left, that you may be successful wherever you go. Keep this Book of the Law always on your lips; meditate on it day and night, so that you may be careful to do everything written in it. Then you will be prosperous and successful. Have I not commanded you? Be strong and courageous. Do not be afraid; do not be discouraged, for the Lord your God will be with you wherever you go.... Whoever rebels against your word and does not obey it, whatever you may command them, will be put to death.

Only be strong and courageous!
—Joshua 1:6–18

Pastor Bowman was so gracious and kind to us. We had the wedding at the church with only our immediate family members in attendance. My dad walked me down the aisle, and Mom cried out, sobbing through the whole thing. She believed that her whole life was ruined because her teenage daughter was pregnant and getting married. The rest of us just tried to ignore her. Bob's parents and grandparents gave us grace and love. They even took us all out to dinner after the wedding. I was finally part of a loving, caring family. And Mercy became my second mom. I went into labor on a hot humid August evening in 1986. In the early hours of the following morning Mike came along and made us a family of three. Bob and I lived with his parents for the first year and half. (I came to love his parents so much that I still consider them to be my second parents today.) Bob and I then got an apartment in a nearby town that was closer to his job. He had landed a very good job right out of high school. We lived in the apartment for six months when we decided to look for a house to buy. We found an old farm house on a few acres only a couple of miles from his parents. The house was perfect for our family and we were ready to have another child.

After we had gotten married, my relationship with God grew by leaps and bounds. Any time the church was open, I was there. I was learning from Pastor Bowman in his Sunday School class, his Sunday sermons, his Sunday night class, and his Wednesday night Bible study. I couldn't get enough of the Bible. I also helped out in the nursery and during the summer at Vacation Bible School. On a Sunday morning while I was pregnant for our second child, I decided to surrender my life to the Lord. I wanted to follow Him one-hundred percent for the rest of my life. I was twenty years old at the time.

In October our baby girl, Summer, made us a family of

four. I had always wanted to be a stay-at-home mom and was very thankful I could do that. I was determined to be a good mother, and I made sure my children knew without a doubt they were loved.

Unfortunately, as I grew closer to God, I grew farther away from Bob. Our relationship was strained, and I had no idea how to handle conflict in a constructive way. The only way I knew was to argue and yell. I did seek counsel at the church, but the leaders there were not on the same page at the time. I was getting mixed messages and became even more confused. One of the counselors told me that it would be a good idea for Bob and I to separate while we tried to mend our marriage. I took her advice and found a small apartment. The kids and I lived in the one bedroom apartment, and I found a job working full-time. The kids were five and two when we ended up going through the divorce. We had been married for six years. I think back on those difficult times of separation and divorce as if they were the best of times, yet the worst of times. The battles were not easy, but they brought me to my knees. My hope was in Christ, and I trusted God would take care of us all. I prayed and I prayed and I prayed.

Through those times, I had become very good friends with an older lady from my church. She became a counselor and confidant. She knew me well and I started calling her "Mom." She seemed to understand my migraines, because she had them also. And I knew her well—or so I thought. I knew that she had struggled at one time with taking narcotics, but she had told me that was all in the past. She had a key to my apartment and would sometimes go there to hang out during the day while her son was at football practice. We trusted each other with our kids and in our homes. Then one day I came home from work and felt that something wasn't right. I went to my cupboard where I kept my pain medications. I could tell that things had been moved around. I had my suspicions and had flushed all of my pain pills down the toliet the night before. So I called and asked her to come over. When I asked her if she had been there during the day, she answered in the affirmative. When I asked if she had been going through my cupboard looking for something, her eyes dropped to the floor. She proceeded to take my key off her keyring and set it on the table. Then she walked out. I never saw her again.

The next three years started off with making the worst decision of my life. I began dating a man named Roger, and after only a few short months (and hoping for a godly male influence for my children), we got married. Within the first few days of being married to him, I knew it was very wrong. Right before my eyes this man I had just married changed into a mean, controlling brute who could overpower me in a split second. He had moved into my little one bedroom apartment and was driving my car that I was making payments on. He would take me to work in the morning and pick me up in the evening. I will always remember the day he finally arrived forty-five minutes late to get me from work. (And I wasn't supposed to be upset because he was out doing "ministry.") Not long after that he got mad at my coworkers. On my day off, he went in, told them I quit and would not be back to work. This was the beginning of my first *Dark Night of the Soul*.

As the weeks turned into months, I felt a dark, heavy cloud form over our home and our relationship. But no matter what was going on in our home, Roger always tried to keep the facade looking good from the outside. Because of his pride, he wouldn't let me work outside of the home. The problem was that he didn't have an income either. He was in "the ministry" and solely relied on contributions to survive. His "ministry" was something he created after writing his first book. Part of his ministry was going into prisons to teach inmates about God, but that was all volunteer work. I went with him into the prisons while we were dating, and I loved it. He and I ministered in almost every prison in the state. Looking back on that time, I can clearly see how I was in love with teaching God's Word but not with the man I had married.

Before we were married, and because I believed in his work at the prisons and with his book, I gave him a large sum of money to pay off the printing of his first book. We were already making plans to marry, so I didn't even think twice about giving it to him. I don't think it is a coincidence that three years later I would have to take out a loan for the exact same amount to pay off my car and start a new life for me and the kids.

Basically, Roger raised money for his ministry by selling books and sharing his story in churches. He self-published his book, and I learned a bit about the publishing process through that three year experience. He did actually take on a "real" job at one point. He took my car and drove to the southern border of Indiana, leaving me and the kids at home in Michigan. Needless to say, the bills started piling up and we had not nearly enough money to cover them. We did not have any health insurance, so each time I went to the ER with a migraine, I got a bill for over one-hundred dollars.

One day out of the blue Roger came home with a bunch of boxes and said that we were moving to a nearby town. I had no idea what was happening. My landlord was putting pressure on us to pay up on the rent. Before we got married, I always paid my rent on time. Roger had found someone to rent us a four bedroom apartment in a nearby town, but after the first month, I don't think he ever paid any rent. At least that rental agreement was in his name and not mine.

At this point I was in a new town with my two young children and no car. I would have to take the kids in the wagon across town to get milk and bread. I also used the wagon to go to the laundromat. Although I did get some child support from Bob, Roger always got the mail at the post office and would make me sign the checks over to him. Then he would cash them to do whatever he was doing with the money. My guess is that he was putting gas in the car and eating out.

After I started college in 1996, I had an English assignment to take a photograph and write an anecdote about it. Here is what I wrote:

A KODAK MOMENT?

It was the summer of 1994 and the kids were overjoyed to be on vacation. The white sand was soft and warm, the sky was crystal clear, and the Atlantic—compelling! In the background there was a brightly colored beach umbrella and beach chairs along with the white capped waves that were rolling in. My children were so excited to see the ocean for the first time. Mike was almost seven and Summer was four. With their feet buried in the sand, they had looked up to say, "Cheese!" Because of his great big grin, one could not miss the fact that Mike had a tooth missing upstairs. It was also evident, when Summer smiled, that she still possessed some baby-fat in her cheeks. We were in New Jersey and everything was perfect.

It was the summer of 1994 and my husband had assured me that this trip was very necessary if we were to meet our financial needs for the near future. As we headed out late at night, the kids nestled down in the back seat to sleep through while we drove to Washington, D.C. I, on the other hand, was very anxious as we started this trip. Although we had enough money for gas and a little food on the way, I did not understand how we would make it back home. Again my husband, a published author, assured me he would be paid for the speaking engagement he was scheduled for in D.C. As a result of the stress from this trip, I ended up giving myself an injection of my pain medicine before we were even out of Michigan. (I felt a Migraine coming on and was hoping the medicine would put a stop to it.) I knew I had one injection left if I needed it during the next few days of our trip.

Late the next day we arrived in D.C. and settled into our rooms. I decided to give myself the other injection—but it was too late. Minutes later I was in agony, began vomiting, and ended up in bed for the next two days. I recall my husband yelling at me for not taking the medicine sooner and for ruining our trip. When I was well enough to travel again, we headed for Pennsylvania to visit his relatives before coming back home. While I had been in bed, my husband went to his engagement, and I was more than interested to know how he had faired financially. "Well," he told me, "they didn't pay me anything, but it was a great experience." This was not the first time I had heard these words, and I was getting very upset. (*How were we to get home?*) He just kept assuring me that everything would be fine, and I should stop nagging him.

While we were in Pennsylvania, his family fed us and put us up for a couple of nights before we needed to head home. The day before we left, his aunt and uncle took us over to New Jersey to see the Atlantic Ocean. My kids were so excited to see the ocean for the first time. They had a great time. (I have always been amazed with the way my children enjoy life—no matter how bad things are around them. Although, I don't think they realized how difficult times were and how unhappy I was.) I remember taking a snapshot as I watched them enjoy the beach. Right after taking the picture, I told everyone that I needed to use the restroom and would be right back. On my way back to the beach from the restroom I was feeling really weak, so I stopped quick for a hot-dog. When I turned back to head for the beach, my husband started yelling at me for taking so long. They were waiting for me so everyone could get some supper. I will never forget the hurt and anger inside of me at that moment. The only problem was that I kept it all inside—again. On the outside I just smiled and apologized for the delay.

I watched a program this summer about women who had been physically abused by their husbands. The pictures of the women, after being beaten, were frightening. These women were having plastic surgery done because many bones had been broken in their faces. The photos showed bruises and swelling so bad that eyes were swollen shut, lips disfigured, and noses that grew back crooked. As I watched the show, it was very evident that these women had been brutally abused. I reflected on my own life and realized that I had many wounds as well. The difference was that my wounds were a result of verbal abuse and were not obvious. I, probably along with many other people in this world, learned how to "put on a face" to cover up the abuse and present the world with a perfect snapshot of myself.

For three years I tried to believe the old saying: "Sticks and stones may break my bones, but names will never hurt me." The truth is that the abusive words hurt me deeply, and now that I am out of the marriage, my wounds are healing. I am so

21

thankful that I don't have to "put on a face" anymore, and that Mike and Summer know for a fact their mommy is happy.

After that trip out East, things only got worse. The landlord was threatening to evict us, and the bank was about to take the car away. It was a very hot summer that year and the migraines were killing me. With no air conditioning in the upstairs apartment, I was miserable. One day I had to swallow my own pride and call Mom to ask for a ride to the ER. Roger was too busy doing "ministry" out on the golf course. He had complete control over me and the little bit of money that did come in. At that point we lacked even enough money to go to the laundromat, so I started washing our clothes in the bathtub. Then our refrigerator died. I was a complete mess. Not to mention that I had become a little mouse of a woman. Everyone around me knew that things were not right. I am usually quite jovial and social. But not for the three years being married to Roger. I completely lost my identity.

Roger had a few male friends who served on the board of his ministry. Basically they were just names on a form he had to fill out to get his 501c3 tax exempt status. One of those board members was Todd. Todd and his family were also good friends of mine. One time I called Todd and asked if he could come over to look at some things. Roger was out of state visiting his mother and asking her for money again. Todd came over, and I pulled out a few boxes of stuff that Roger had brought into the marriage. They basically contained old receipts and paperwork. But they were just tossed into the boxes in no organized manner. I had gone through the boxes when Roger was not at home and saw numerous utility shut off notices, eviction notices, and even child support papers that showed he owed the state of Washington over $13,000. Those items really upset me, and I needed someone I trusted to help me make sense of everything. But what really upset me was when the phone rang, and it was Roger. I motioned to Todd that it was him. Roger proceeded to yell at me and ask, "Who is there? What are you doing?" I played dumb, but it freaked me out. Somehow he always found out what I was doing and who I was talking to when he was not around. I started to think that he had the apartment bugged.

One Sunday morning Roger and I, along with the kids, were in the car driving two hours away for church. He was scheduled to give his testimony at the service and try to sell some books. All the way there (the whole two hours) he screamed at me and said horrible things to me. I was in tears just sitting there. I was trapped. As we were pulling into the church parking lot, he told me to stop crying and wipe the tears away. He wanted to make sure I put on a good face for his presentation. The kids and I were sitting in the front row of the church that morning when Roger introduced us and said that he and I had a great marriage. What a joke!

Roger was in the middle of writing his second book when we got married, and he told me that I would be doing all of the word processing from his hand written pages. But it didn't matter how fast or how well I was doing the work, he was never happy. He would often tell me to do it better, and I was just plain stupid. He didn't have anything nice to say about me unless we were around other people.

He was able to finish his second book while we were married and had it printed. I don't remember how he paid for the printing, but one day he started bringing in box after box after box of books. The boxes lined the entire hallway stacked almost to the ceiling and along one wall in the living room. I was so scared of him and felt trapped. One day he got so mad at me that he flipped the coffee table across the room. He had poured himself a huge bowl of cereal and milk and set it on the table. That all went flying along with the table. That was the moment I knew I needed to get out.

At this point Bob was being laid off from work quite often, so there were weeks when I would not get a child support check. In order to get around Roger taking my child support money, I finally had the checks rerouted to Mom's house. He didn't know any better because Bob wasn't getting paid very often. Thankfully, I had several checks waiting for me when I did leave Roger. Since I believed that I did not have grounds for a divorce, I was simply planning to be separated. Once again swallowing my pride, I called Mom and asked if the kids and I could stay with her until an apartment became available. She then arranged for a couple of her guy friends to come help me move my stuff, because I didn't want to drag any of our friends into the situation. I was very depressed and just needed out. The day we were loading the moving truck, Roger came home from who knows where and thankfully left the car with me.

Speaking of my mom's house, I say that because my dad had recently divorced her. After thirty-six years, he had called it quits. He told me that he should have divorced her twenty years prior. I don't understand why he didn't.

Anyway, my first order of business was to get my car paid off. That is when I went to a family friend who lent me the money. Now the car was mine, and I didn't have to worry about that. It only took three weeks to get into an apartment, and I was glad to move out of Mom's basement. This would be my seventh move since I was seventeen. I was ready to start a new life and stay in one place for awhile. And I knew the kids needed some stability.

Of course Roger was angry about me leaving, and he continued to threaten divorce if I didn't do what he said. I told him that I did not plan to file, but if he felt the need, so be it. In regards to the marriage, I prayed and asked God to give me direction. And He did. He gave me two words: *Do Nothing.* So that's what I did. I focused on settling into my two bedroom apartment with my kids. I enrolled them in the school that was right in our neighborhood. Mike was starting third grade and Summer was starting kindergarten. I was feeling the dark cloud being lifted off of me, and I could start breathing again.

I was referred to a little old Christian lady who might help me through this time. Her name was Echo. She was such a blessing to me. She told me not to go back into that abusive relationship. She hugged on me and told me that God was still with me. At the time I left Roger, I was devastated emotionally, financially, spiritually, and mentally. Echo was the little light that I held onto. Years later I went back to thank her, but she was nowhere to be found. I truly believe God had sent me an angel named Echo.

In order to be involved with the school, I started attending and participating in the school's Parent Teacher Organization. It was there that I met a new friend. She was looking for some help with childcare after school until her and her husband would get home from work. It was a great way for me to start earning an income, yet still be with my kids before and after school. Then I started applying to all of the elementary schools in town for a paraprofessional teacher aid position. Not long after, I got a call to be a substitute teacher aide for the day. I didn't even know that was a thing. God changed my world that day. I'll never forget walking into a classroom with the kids after lunch and hearing an audible voice saying, "You can do this! You can be a teacher." I was blown away! I had never even considered teaching school. But God was in it, and I signed up for college classes the next day.

I was providing childcare for the two children after school; I had a part-time position as a paraprofessional, and I started taking college classes. In regards to the marriage, I did nothing. It wasn't too long before I got papers in the mail. I was a little surprised, because Roger didn't have money for a lawyer, yet the paperwork came from a lawyer's office. There was a hearing scheduled, and on that day, I went to the courthouse. I took along my school books and planned on studying until our case came up. A lawyer came into the room and introduced himself as Roger's lawyer. But no Roger. I thought that was strange, but I politely listened to what the lawyer had to say. He gave me a piece of paper and asked me to sign it. I asked what the paper was for? He explained that Roger had changed his mind. He did not want to go through with the divorce. I remembered those two words: *Do Nothing*, and I asked, "What if I don't sign it?" The lawyer was taken aback and said, "Roger didn't tell me this might happen. Let me go talk to the judge." A few minutes later the lawyer returned and said the judge would like to see me in his chambers. So I went in. He asked me to explain what was going on. I told him about the abuse and how Roger had threatened divorce numerous times throughout our marriage. The judge said, "This is crazy. You will be divorced today." I was so happy to be released from the grip that Roger had on me. It was 1996 and I was twenty-eight years old. I had been married and divorced twice, had two children, and continued to praise my Lord.

FOUR

College, Church & Children

And who knows but that you have come to
your royal position for such a time as this?
—Esther 4:14

I won't say it was easy to praise the Lord through all of the tough times, but it sure did help me get through. After the divorce from Roger, I started looking for a new church in my hometown where I was living. I knew I needed a church that was soundly based on the Bible, and I needed the people to be accepting of me and where I was at in life. One day I ran into a friend at the grocery store, and she recommended a church called Adams Lake Church. I had heard of that church but was very skeptical because of things I had heard. Later that same day, I was talking with another friend who recommended the same church and told me how much she loved it. I took that as a sign and agreed with God that I would go for a few weeks and see what it was like. I would sneak in the door and slip into the back row of the sanctuary and just observe. Then I would slip back out the same way before anyone could see me. I was still very depressed and beaten down. There was a lot of healing that needed to take place before I could engage with a church family again.

After slipping in and out of that church for two years, God nudged me and said, "It's time. You are healed, and this is your church." The first thing I did was sign up for nursery duty. I love taking care of babies, and my children would come in and help me on the weeks when it was my turn. The next thing I did was call a man named James who was the leader of the drama team. I had seen these three to five minute skits the team would do each week before the sermon, and everyone seemed to be having such a good time. When I talked to James, he told me that they would be happy to have me join. I could come the following Monday evening to drama practice and introduce myself to everyone. So I did. And it was love at first sight. At first sight of the team that is. Everyone was so warm and accepting of me. They seemed more like a family than a team.

The next five years found me attending drama practice every Monday night. And soon after I started coming, James put me on stage to do a scene with one of the guys. Was I nervous? Of course! But I had my lines down pat and felt very comfortable with the role I would be playing of a woman at a job interview. It went on without a hitch. Once again I was in love. With the stage that is. James continued to teach me about acting, and he really drew the talent out of me. I didn't even know it was there. James was an amazing leader and teacher. And so my church family started growing, and those on my drama team became my closest friends.

My weekly schedule was full, and I was feeling like myself again. I loved going to college and learning as much as I could. I dug into my Bible, started learning from there again, and I was really enjoying my job at the elementary school. I was able to work part-time around my college schedule, and that was great. I'll never forget a conversation I had with one of my coworkers. She told me I would find the right man someday who would take good care of me. Hah! I told her there was no way I would ever get married again. No way!

I was still getting child support, and thankfully it was coming regularly again. But even with my part-time wage and doing childcare, money was very tight. I kept a strict budget and was adamant about providing for my children the best I could. They never went without food or clothes. My work was across town from the school they attended, but I kept very involved and volunteered at their school as much as possible.

It was so much fun being in a writing class and learning how to write better. After receiving a package in the mail one day, I wrote this:

THE GIFT
(December 1999)

A package came for me today
with no return address.
I was feeling blue and a bit depressed
when I said, "Hmmm—wonder what this could be."

Sometimes it's tough being both Mom and Dad
and there is doubt as to what is the best.
The past few days had been filled
with concern and feelings of failure.

These feelings faded as I opened the gift
and read the note inside.
The small box contained a dainty chain
adorned with a simple gold cross.

The note was simple, yet profound.
It began: "Daughter, I know that this small
token of my love for you…"
and continued on to offer encouragement.

This lovely message was sent to me
to show love, grace and pride in
a job well done. "Keep up the awesome work"
was the final request.

Following the few words that brought
tears to my eyes, the note was signed:
Love, Your Heavenly Father

A year later, I was given another gift. This time it was an envelope that one of the church ladies handed to me on a Sunday morning. This is what I wrote:

ANOTHER GIFT
(December 2000)

Last year at this time it was
a box full of love that was sent my way.

A chain I still hold dear and a note
that still encourages me each new day.

I know my Lord is faithful

as I strive to do His will.

And once again it is December
and He has sent another gift.

The past few weeks were filled with prayer,
as I tried not to worry.

Just had to put my trust in Him
to see me through the year.

This gift also had no return address,
just a small yellow envelope with my name simply printed.

Thinking it was probably a holiday card,
I tossed it on the seat and almost forgot it was there.

As I returned home and took it in with my stuff,
I opened that small yellow envelope:

Three one-hundred dollar bills it contained—
and another prayer was answered.

"Thank you, Lord!" was all I could say
as I remembered His love, grace and faithfulness.

Another gift has come my way
and I'm sure it was sent from Heaven
(with love) from my Heavenly Father!

It had been five years since we moved into the two-bedroom apartment in my hometown. Summer and I were sharing the master bedroom, but we were both ready for our own space. I decided to start looking for a three-bedroom home for rent.

One afternoon I went to look at a home out in the country that was only one mile from our church. The visit went very well, and the house was great. I came home and told the kids that I had looked at a house close to the church. I said, "But there are two issues that you may not like. First, what would be Mike's bedroom is very small. He would have room for his bed and dresser and that is it. The other two bedrooms are upstairs. Summer, I would give you the bigger bedroom, but you would have to walk through my room to get to it." They both said the house sounded great and were anxious to go look at it. Then Mike said, "It sounds good to me—unless there is a pond there. Then I'm in one-hundred percent and don't need to go look at it." My jaw dropped and his eyes lit up like no tomorrow when I told him that it did indeed have a pond. I can assure you that for the five years we lived in that house, a lot of fish were caught out of that pond.

About the same time we moved into the house, I graduated from the community college Summa Cum Laude with a GPA of 3.96. I was thrilled to say the least. Then it was time to decide on a good four year college that had a teaching program. I visited a few but knew for sure which one I liked the best. It was a small college about forty-five minutes from our house. When I visited, it was like everyone on campus was a family. Then I went to the office of the person who collects the tuition. Talk about sticker shock! This gentleman told me that with my GPA and income, I would qualify for several scholarships. But the rest of the money would have to come out of my pocket. It was not an easy decision by any means, but I finally decided to go to Groving College full-time for two years to get my teaching degree. I would take out student loans to help pay for tuition and to help feed my family.

I made some great friends in those two years, and I'm

still in touch with a few. The final semester was my student teaching experience, and then I would be a certified teacher. The beginning of my third semester started out just like the first two. I drove the forty-five minutes to school but decided to turn off my radio and spend some time talking with God that day. I felt the need to pray for all of my family members individually as well as friends and colleagues. Once I arrived at the school, I walked up to my chemistry class just like I had done the past two weeks. Only that day was different. As we were gathering into the classroom, someone mentioned that a plane had just hit a building in New York. Our professor didn't think too much about it and went on to teach the class. But as class went on, someone came in and told us that there was another plane that had just hit the same building. At that moment, time stood still. People were walking around dumb founded. Instead of going to the library to study for the rest of the day, I headed back home. On my way, I decided to stop at Brett and Mercy's house to turn on the TV. Everything I was hearing on the radio was all so confusing and dreadful. I needed to see what was going on. That was the day our world changed forever, and it simply became known as 911.

FIVE

My Career?

There was a time when I packed my dreams away.
There was a time when I was so afraid.
I thought I'd reached the end,
I am made of more than my yesterdays.
And I have the courage like never before, yeah.
I've settled for less now I'm ready for more,
My fears behind me, gone are the shadows and doubts.
That was then, this is my now.
—*This is my Now* by Jordin Sparks

It was exciting to be graduating from Groving College with my Bachelor's Degree in Elementary Education. I ended up with a GPA of 3.96. I was so happy and wanted a big celebration at the house. I wanted to thank everyone for their help along the way. I would start my student teaching the next semester, and I couldn't be more ready.

I had decided to do my student teaching with one of the second grade teachers from the school where I had been working. She was a seasoned teacher and was a master at classroom management. That was the part I was the most insecure about. I knew I could learn a lot from her over that semester. We started in the fall and everything was great. Until the first of November. That was when the principal called me into her office. I sat down, and she proceeded to tell me about a fifth grade position that would be available soon. One of her teachers needed to retire per her doctor for health reasons. The principal asked if the college would allow me to take over the class before the end of the semester? I wasn't sure, but I would surely find out!

My college professors were ecstatic about my job offer. They were more than willing to let me do that. I had to say goodbye to the second graders but told them I would be just down the hall at the other end of the building. I stepped into teaching fifth grade full-time the Monday after the Thanksgiving holiday. I was stepping into a pair of shoes of another master teacher. She was incredible. The transition was so smooth, and the kids didn't miss a beat. I was in my element, my dream had come true, and my hard work had paid off. Or at least I thought it had.

In January 2003 the educational system in our state changed forever. "No Child Left Behind" was legislation that went into effect on January 1st. It was that day when school districts all over Michigan started scrambling to figure out how to balance their budgets. Needless to say, teachers in every district were getting pink slips (their walking papers.) We had two first year teachers in our school, and they both got the boot. But I was considered a long-term substitute and didn't have a chance. The principal apologized to me numerous times because she really wanted me to stay on. A little after six months of teaching fifth grade, my very short career came to an end. Over the next five years I would go to every school district in our area of Michigan and apply for teaching positions. The problem was that nobody was hiring, and budget cuts continued to be made. I was able to collect unemployment at least, but that didn't last very long. I finally found a position working for a building contractor as a receptionist.

My time at that job is a story in and of itself. My employer was very difficult. He could be very mean and would often fly off the handle at any one of us in the office. Whenever someone was asked to meet him in his office, we would refer to it as them being "summoned into the black hole." We wouldn't see them again for hours. He would just talk and talk and talk. My job at the office was to greet clients and answer the phone. I was bored stiff. When the weather was nice, I would take a walk over my lunch break. The office was situated in a beautiful office park with ponds, trails, and beautiful landscape.

My kids at the time were in high school and middle school. They were very busy with friends, at their extra curricular activities, and working part-time jobs after school. I had started developing some new friendships at the church. A new singles group had formed, and we decided to have our first event at my house. It was fall, so we had a cookout, bon fire, and hayride. It was a blast. It was the beginning of many lasting friendships. That evening everyone had gone home except one of my girlfriends and a new guy. We sat around the fire talking and getting to know one another. The new guy, Tony, asked me some questions about raising my kids that I didn't know how to answer. I just brushed it off and changed the subject.

The next morning at work I started wrestling with those questions he had asked. On my lunch break I went outside to walk. As I walked, I prayed. I felt that God wanted me to call Tony and ask him to get together sometime. I was not happy. As a matter of fact, I argued with God the whole hour I was out there. Before I went back into the office, I finally said to God, "Fine. I'll call him. But he had better say no." That night I went home and called Tony. He seemed happy to hear from me. I asked him if we could talk about what we had been discussing the night before. He said, "Sure! But I have to run a friend up to town first. Can I call you back in a few?" I was fine with that and hoped he wouldn't call back. But he did. I finally got up the guts to ask if he would like to get together sometime. He said, "Sure! How about I pick you up at 7:00 Friday night?"

I was in shock. I had been happily single for ten years and didn't want to do the dating thing again. It was NOT on my agenda. But God's agenda took precedence again. So we went out and had a great time. And I was smitten. Tony and I dated for two years.

While dating Tony, I read a couple of books by John and Stasi Eldredge called *Wild at Heart* and *Captivating*. These books changed everything for me. They helped me learn and understand how God creates men and women with very different purposes in mind. That each gender must stay in his or her role or else they won't be able to function the way God has intended. I highly recommend that everyone read these two books to get a better understanding of who you are and to better understand those around you.

I love the way Eldredge explains how "in the heart of every man is a desperate desire for a battle to fight, an adventure to live, and a beauty to rescue." Stasi explains that "We think you'll find that every woman in her heart of hearts longs for three things: to be romanced, to play an irreplaceable role in a great adventure, and to unveil beauty. That's what makes a woman come alive." My favorite passage from these books is one that resonated deep in my heart because I thought, "No way. This stuff only happens in fairytales." I never thought something like this was even possible: "A woman in the presence of a good man, a real man, loves being a woman. His strength allows her feminine heart to flourish. His pursuit draws out her beauty. And a man in the presence of a real woman loves being a man. Her beauty arouses him to play the man, it draws out his strength. She inspires him to be the hero. Would that we all were so fortunate."

Of course my relationship with Tony was on my mind as I read these books. And I was beginning to believe there might really be men out there who are decent human beings. Unfortunately, our relationship didn't last. But—I did learn a lot over those two years. I was heartbroken, yes. But God had other plans. So once again I surrendered to His will. And I thanked God for the time Tony and I had together. Not only did I learn a lot, but I decided that I would rather have loved and lost than to never have loved at all.

Back to my job as a receptionist: I had been working there for about a year when one of my coworkers came to me looking confused. It was his job to open the mail everyday and deliver each piece to those in the office. He came to me with a credit card bill that didn't make sense. After looking it over, I had to agree that it was a very strange bill from a company we did not have any accounts with. I decided to have another coworker come up to my desk to see what she thought. Jamie worked in the accounting department and she was confused by the bill as well.

Jamie and I decided to keep this information to ourselves,

and she started looking into the accounts and all transactions. A couple of days later we had come to the conclusion that the CFO of the company had opened the account without authorization. She and I called the boss into the conference room and told him about our discoveries. He was shocked. After a complete investigation, it was determined that the CFO had stolen hundreds of thousands of the company's money.

After accessing the now current financial situation with his company, the boss started to let people go. It was a real let down when Jamie and I were told that we had to go. We were quite disappointed that we had done all the work to prove what the CFO had done, yet we were being let go. I wasn't too worried about being without work though, because the boss was so difficult and I was so bored at that job.

So started my job search again. Keep in mind that I was still looking for a teaching position also. I was debating going back to college to get my Master's Degree. But that would mean taking out more loans. Bottom line—I just couldn't rationalize more loans. Not long after having a few interviews, I had two job offers. One was in a dental office and one was for a receptionist in the office of a manufacturing business. For various reasons, I chose the receptionist. It was about a forty-five minute drive from home, but I really enjoyed the position.

While I was working at this new receptionist position, Mike was ready to graduate from high school. It was the spring of 2005, and we had a great celebration with all of our friends and family. The only problem with him graduating was the cut in my child support. I would only be getting support for Summer from that point on. That took a huge hit to my budget. So once again I needed to make some tough decisions. As a family we decided that Mike would go live with Brett and Mercy, Summer and I would move to an apartment closer to my job, and she would change schools to finish out her high school years. She had saved enough money from her after school job to buy a car. And then she found a new job not too far from the apartment. The rent was less and I could once again balance the budget.

We had only been living in that apartment for a few months before I needed to make another tough decision. Summer would get home from school before me and would let herself into the apartment. The problem was that she believed a guy was stalking her. She was scared stiff. She said that he would be watching for her to come home and then follow her into the building. On two separate occasions she called me at work, and I raced home. I got the police involved, but one day I came home and she was under her bed with a butcher knife. She was shaking. Another problem was the violence at her school. It was getting worse and she was not feeling safe there either. She and I decided to move back to my hometown and find an apartment that I could afford. This would be my eleventh move. I was getting dizzy, but was becoming very good at packing and efficient at moving.

About the same time we were back and forth between apartments, my son's girlfriend got pregnant, and they made plans to get married. Mike was working a good job, and after the wedding he moved into her parents' house. My granddaughter was born in September of 2006, and I couldn't be more thrilled to be a grandmother.

Soon after Tony and I broke up, I decided to start dating again. I had to do something to get my mind off of him. I needed to move on. And I had also decided that I would consider marriage again only if the right man came along. I went to the internet looking for love. Online dating was just becoming popular, and I thought I'd give it a try. I ended up dating several different men, and some of them were really nice guys. Maybe there was hope for a relationship again in my future.

Once we got settled again, I decided to start looking for a new job. My current one was not a good atmosphere anymore. And I was frustrated that I did not get the new position I was hoping for. Instead, the boss's daughter was hired, and I had to train her to do the job that I thought should have been given to me. I ended up taking a job working in a hospital. It was for a desk clerk in the ICU units. I would be working the night shift 7pm–7am, three days a week.

In the spring of that year I went to my tax man with all of the necessary paperwork to file my income tax return. I was dumbfounded when he handed me the return and told me that I owed $500. I told him that there must have been some mistake. I begged him to look things over again because I had always gotten a refund before. So he did. But I really did owe the $500. I was distraught knowing there was no way I could pay that. I was barely making ends meet as it was. Seeking the advice of a family friend, who worked in the investment business, was the only thing I could think of. This friend looked over my budget and said he didn't see anything else I could do.

After much prayer and petitioning, I decided to move out of my apartment and try to rent a room from someone. And I would have Summer go to Brett and Mercy's to live while she finished high school.

The next series of events were nothing short of a miracle. My mom and step-dad had recently purchased a new condo across town. And the gentleman who purchased their previous condo was living in Arizona. Mom mentioned that he might let me stay in the condo since he wasn't using it. I figured it was worth a try. She gave me his phone number and I called. I told Ron my situation and how his condo was just a block away from the apartment I was currently living in. The conversation I had with Ron that day on the phone, in a parking lot, near the river, left me speechless. And that doesn't happen very often! I found out that he had yet to get the keys to the place because the purchase was finalized after he was back in Arizona. When I asked him why he bought a condo here in Michigan when he was living in Arizona, he said that he wanted a place to stay when he came to visit his family. I could hear the compassion in his voice when he told me that I was more than welcome to stay in the condo as long as I needed. He asked if my mom still had a key to the place and I said, "Yes." When I asked how much rent he would charge me, he said, "No. You don't have to pay me anything. And you can move in as soon as possible." I was in tears. An elderly man who didn't know me or anything about me was allowing me to live in his home while he was still in Arizona. He told me that he was planning to come back to Michigan in a few weeks to visit, and we could meet one another then. God had sent me another angel!

This time I didn't have much stuff to move, because I had sold off most of my furniture and household items trying to get enough money to pay the IRS. Basically I had my bed, a dresser, some dishes, and my clothes. The singles group helped me move again. Everything fit in the back of a pickup, and we only had to go one block up the street.

I would talk with Ron several more times on the phone before we met. He had such a giving heart. When I would ask him why he let me live there, he simply said, "I like to pay it forward. God has blessed me so much." This man not only let me live in his condo rent free, but he also paid for all of the utilities while I was there. When he did come back to visit, he went downtown and purchased a stove, a washer and a dryer for me to use. As we talked, I began to unfold my life story to him up to that point. We became good friends. I knew I could never repay him for his generosity, but I did promise to pay it forward in the future as I was able. It ended up that I stayed in his condo for several months before I made another huge decision.

Ron was not only helping me with my immediate needs, his compassion overflowed with wanting to help me with my long-term needs. It concerned him that I still had my Michigan teaching certificate but was unable to get a teaching position. He started looking to the schools in Arizona to find out about the possibility for a teaching position there. He found out that Arizona was screaming for teachers to come and fill the needs of the growing population. He lived in the Pheonix area and found several possible school districts there that were looking for teachers. I got really excited thinking that maybe God's plan was for me to get my dream job and start my career with teaching out there. But if I was going to do it, I had to act fast. My Michigan certification would be expiring soon. If I waited too long, I wouldn't be able to transfer my certificate to Arizona.

Ron was back in Arizona, and we made plans for me to come visit him for a week to go job hunting. He flew me out to Phoenix where I would spend the next week weaving through the red tape to get an Arizona certificate. Then I visited several schools and left my resume. We got a lot accomplished in that week. I flew back home to wait for my certificate to come in the mail.

I was beyond excited when it did arrive. As I was doing my research and applying for jobs, I found a career fair that was going to be held at the University in Pheonix, and it was just for school districts searching for potential teachers. Once again Ron flew me out there for a long weekend to attend the career fair and to visit more of the schools. And that is what I did. Then I came home and waited. It wasn't long at all before an administrator from one of the districts in the area called and asked if I could do a phone interview with him and one of his principals. They offered me the job on the spot. But I would have to come out by the end of December to start teaching after the Christmas and New Year break.

The first grade position needed to be filled quickly because the teacher who was in that room had decided not to come back to work after the break. She had been driving two hours each way to get to work every day. She had gotten into a bad car accident that made her rethink her commute. Similar to my fifth grade position, I would be stepping into the shoes of the previous teacher who had started the year with those students.

Once again I would be packing up, moving, and taking on a new job. Keep in mind that I never made these life changing decisions without a lot of soul searching and prayer. I always felt God working in each decision, and I was doing my best to follow His will. Taking the position in Arizona would make my eleventh job change. Through it all, I had learned a little bit about a lot of things, but I was a master at none. That really bothered me, and I was ready to finally settle into a career.

I was able to give my two weeks notice at the hospital, and everyone was excited for me. My friends pitched in to help—again; I was packed and ready to roll out the driveway on Christmas morning 2007. Summer would continue staying with Brett and Mercy to finish out her senior year. Mike and his family were now living in an apartment and doing well. Leaving them behind was the hardest part, but I promised that I would be able to come back for visits, and we would keep in touch via phone and computer.

This move was huge for me. I had never lived outside of West Michigan, let alone any other state. The next few days found me and a friend driving the 2,000 miles to my new home. Ron had lined up an apartment for me and had paid the deposit and the first month's rent. All I had to do was drive to the complex, pick up the key, and I would be in. "Are you nervous about moving so far away?" people kept asking me. I wasn't nervous or anxious at all. I had complete faith that this was God's plan, and I was at peace. As we drove those miles over the next three days, my friend kept asking me if I was ok. Was I getting anxious about such a huge step? Each time I truthfully answered, "I am fine. I'm not feeling anything but peace."

But when we arrived at the apartment, and started unloading the truck, it hit me. I was overwhelmed with the thoughts and feelings of being in this foreign land all by myself and having to navigate without the support of family and friends. Instantly I missed my kids and family members. I wouldn't see them again for five, long, difficult months. I sobbed and said, "What have I just done?!?!"

My friend stayed with me that first night, and it was heart wrenching to say goodbye the next morning. My friend tried to assure me that if this didn't work out, I could always go back home to Michigan. Those words stayed with me. I wasn't sure how I would get along, but was determined to make it work.

And so began my second *Dark Night of the Soul*. (The first one was when I was married to Roger.) I felt completely lost and was so terribly lonely. Sadness loomed over me as I started getting depressed. My first few days were spent unpacking, buying food at the next door grocery, and calling home to talk to family and friends. I also prepared the best I could for my first days of teaching. I didn't drive to the school until the first of January 2008. The principal was meeting me at the school to let me into my classroom to set things up. I would have three days to get everything ready.

I'll never forget that day. The principal introduced herself and welcomed me to the school. She was pleasant and showed me down a hallway. She said, "Just walk to the end of this hall and turn left. Your room will be the third door on your left. The custodian has unlocked the door for you. If you need anything, he will be around to help." That was it. She turned around and walked out leaving me standing there. She didn't show me around the school or walk me to my room. She didn't show me where anything was or ask if I had any questions. That was it.—She just left me standing there.

I took my bag and headed down the empty, ominous hallway. When I got to my door, I slowly opened it with a brief feeling of excitement. I had been excited to see what the students had been learning. I wanted to see the word wall that is in every first grade classroom. (It is a list on a bulletin board of all the words the kids had mastered in reading and writing so far.) I looked forward to seeing the alphabet, the instructional calendar, the number line, and maybe some of their artwork displayed around the room. My excitement turned to horror the moment I opened the door and walked in. What I saw was WHITE. Just white. No color, no bulletin boards, no word wall, no alphabet—just white walls, white floors, white desks and chairs. There was one bookshelf with some textbooks. There was a teacher desk with a computer. But when I went over to what was now my desk, all I could find was a stapler—with no staples.

Lowering my head to the desk, I started weeping. What in the world had I done? God, what am I supposed to do? Several years earlier I had collected a lot of items that I could have used in this classroom, but I had given it all away to other teachers because I didn't think I would ever have the opportunity to teach again. It felt like I was in a nightmare. I had no idea of where to start. And I only had three days to figure it out. The other teacher hadn't even left her lesson plans. I had no idea in the world of where these students were at academically. I had no idea of what chapters or lessons to start with.

I decided to start with the administrator who hired me. When I reached him on the phone, I asked if he could come over to the school. He was almost as surprised as I was that the other teacher had left nothing. Apparently, everything she had taken with her was her own stuff. He said he would see what he could do and get back to me. He was able to get one-hundred dollars for me to go to the Teacher Store across town. One hundred dollars. Period. Well, I tried to get the most important stuff, but ended up having to use some of my own money to buy a number line, alphabet, teaching calendar, a couple of informational posters—that was it. I also went home and gathered some household items that I could use. A poster, some baskets—then I went to a local Salvation Army store to find a beanbag chair for the reading corner and some books—that was it. That's all I had to work with. I spent most of the next forty-eight hours in my classroom trying to prepare for Monday when the kids would come in. I wasn't nearly as prepared as I had hoped, but they came anyway.

My saving grace while teaching was two of the other first grade teachers. They became my support team as I struggled to get things going. We became good friends, and they helped me out many times. We collaborated well.

I had been working for about three weeks and was looking forward to getting my first paycheck on Friday. My rent was due, and I needed to get that paid. But—no paycheck. I was once again in shock. How could I not be getting my paycheck? Apparently there had been some mistake made at the administration office. They would do what they could to try and cut my check on Monday. In the meantime I was out of money and really, really angry. If I remember correctly, it was the middle of the next week before I actually got the check.

It wasn't long before I realized I needed help with more than just my classroom. My depression was starting to affect my work. Whenever I would see a photo of my kids or granddaughter on my screensaver, I would start crying. So I went to see a doctor who was recommended to me. The medicine helped, but I still struggled. After school every day I was having to stay until late into the evening to prepare for the next day. Then I took papers home with me to grade before falling asleep. I had no life outside of work. That would have been fine with me if I had a decent job. But it was just one disaster after another.

I had asked my principal if I could get some help with classroom management. Being in Arizona meant that we had families moving in and out of our district constantly. On a weekly basis I would have a whole different set of kids to teach. I had a hard enough time learning all thirty-two names, let alone where each one was at with reading and math. It was like having a revolving door with kids coming and going each week. My principal arranged to have a mentor come in and help with what she could. This gal set up a day when I could go visit another school and just observe another first grade classroom. She was going to set up a substitute teacher for my class that day. When that day came, I drove straight to the other school and found the teacher I would be observing. Just like I did everyday, I turned off my cell phone and put it into my purse. The day went well, and I took as many notes as I could. It was actually refreshing to see a master teacher at work.

At the end of the school day, I thanked the teacher and went out to my car. I pulled out my phone to turn it back on, and it was blowing up with voicemails. It was my principal asking where I was and why I didn't show up for work that morning. She left several very disheartening messages. She was not happy. I on the other hand was like, "What in the world?" I drove straight over there and went into her office. Before she could start in on me, I said there was supposed to be a substitute. That so-and-so was supposed to have set that up for me, etc. She didn't seem to believe me until she called my mentor and asked. Oops. She forgot to schedule a sub for the day. Too late now. It would have been nice to get an apology—but that did not happen.

Needless to say, that was my worst work experience ever. Anything that could go wrong did go wrong. About half-way through the semester, one of my teacher friends introduced me to a song that I had never heard. As soon as it started playing, I broke down and wept uncontrollably. The song is called *Home* by Michael Buble. Here is some of it:

> "Another airplane
> I'm just too far from where you are
> And I know just why you could not come along
> with me
> That this was not your dream
> And I'm surrounded by
> A million people
> I still feel alone
> Oh, let me go home"

I could have written this song myself. I missed my family so much and could not wait to see them. So toward the end of the semester I started asking God if I could just go back home to Michigan? His answer was a resounding, "Yes, you can." My desert experience (literally and figuratively) was coming to an end. I was confused though and asked God where would I live when I got there? What about work? I only had a little bit of money saved up, and I needed that to get home for my daughter's high school graduation, and then back again to get my belongings. This is what I sensed God telling me: "I've always taken care of your needs. I will continue to provide. Just trust me." So that's what I did.

SIX

Marriage Again?

Only once in your life, I truly believe, you find someone who can completely turn your world around. You tell them things that you've never shared with another soul and they absorb everything you say and actually want to hear more. You share hopes for the future, dreams that will never come true, goals that were never achieved and the many disappointments life has thrown at you. When something wonderful happens, you can't wait to tell them about it, knowing they will share in your excitement. They are not embarrassed to cry with you when you are hurting or laugh with you when you make a fool of yourself. Never do they hurt your feelings or make you feel like you are not good enough, but rather they build you up and show you the things about yourself that make you special and even beautiful. There is never any pressure, jealousy or competition but only a quiet calmness when they are around. You can be yourself and not worry about what they will think of you because they love you for who you are. The things that

51

seem insignificant to most people such as a note, song or walk become invaluable treasures kept safe in your heart to cherish forever. Memories of your childhood come back and are so clear and vivid it's like being young again. Colors seem brighter and more brilliant. Laughter seems part of daily life where before it was infrequent or didn't exist at all. A phone call or two during the day helps to get you through a long day's work and always brings a smile to your face. In their presence, there's no need for continuous conversation, but you find you're quite content in just having them nearby. Things that never interested you before become fascinating because you know they are important to this person who is so special to you. You think of this person on every occasion and in everything you do. Simple things bring them to mind like a pale blue sky, gentle wind or even a storm cloud on the horizon. You open your heart knowing that there's a chance it may be broken one day and in opening your heart, you experience a love and joy that you never dreamed possible. You find that being vulnerable is the only way to allow your heart to feel true pleasure that's so real it scares you. You find strength in knowing you have a true friend and possibly a soul mate who will remain loyal to the end. Life seems completely different, exciting and worthwhile. Your only hope and security is in knowing that they are a part of your life.

—Bob Marley

It was a Thursday night in late May when I boarded the red eye flight back to Michigan. My baby girl was graduating from high school on Friday, and there was no way I was missing it. It was a glorious reunion with the kids, and we were all filled with emotion. I was home. I stayed in Michigan for a week before flying back to Arizona to get my stuff. That week we celebrated Summer's graduation with another party. I was one proud and happy mama.

Before I had left Arizona to come back, I had a few conversations with my son. He told me that he had an extra bedroom in his apartment that I could use until I could get a place of my own. I could even use his computer to search for jobs. So that was the plan. But then there was one conversation that was not so positive. He told me about a summons he had gotten in the mail from the county clerk's office. He was to show up for a hearing in a few weeks because my mom was suing him for $1,500. I didn't want to believe it, but I did. That sounded exactly like something my mom would do. You see, Mike had bought a car from my mom and step-dad a few years earlier. He was to make monthly payments until it was paid off. But then Mike got laid off from work and was not bringing in much income. He had fallen behind in payments the past couple of months. He asked me what he should do. I said, "Don't do anything until I get back. We will deal with it then."

So after the graduation ceremony, we headed out to Brett and Mercy's and sat down with them. We explained the situation and asked if they could in any way help him out. We didn't even finish the conversation before Brett handed him a check for $1,500 and said, "Pay her and be done with it." That's what grandparents are supposed to do! I told Mike to get a money order or cashiers check and have it sent to Mom via certified mail. And he did.

After the graduation ceremony and party, Summer and I flew back to Arizona to bring back my car and my stuff. Our trip back to Michigan was my gift to her and we took our time, stopping to sightsee along the way. In Arizona we visited the red rock country, a couple of ghost towns, and The Grand Canyon. We then headed east, and one of our adventures was to explore Graceland. I wasn't sure if she would enjoy it, but she really did have a good time there. We took a week to make the trip, and it was one of the best things I have ever done. It was a wonderful time of mother/daughter bonding and just being together. We had missed each other immensely.

Once I was back in my hometown, staying with my son, I jumped right back into the singles group and hanging out with my friends. As a group we planned a get together at one of the local parks. We decided to open up our group to any single person from the community. They would be welcome to join us for a cookout and see what the group was all about. I wrote up an article, and with a photo of our core group, had it published in the weekly local newspaper. We wanted people to be able to call us if they had any questions, so I listed my phone as a contact number.

A couple of days after the article was published, I got a phone call. I was so surprised when I answered and heard James's voice on the other end. Remember my friend James who was my drama leader at the church? He told me he had seen my photo and phone number in the newspaper. He decided to call and see what was going on in my life. I said that it was way more than I could tell him over the phone that evening. So we decided to meet for dinner a few days later and get caught up. He had also told me that his wife had recently left him and they had gotten a divorce.

I tried to console him, but it seemed like he was doing fairly well by this point. The next day I got called for a job interview. When I went in, I was hired on the spot. "Thank you, Lord." was all I could say. He was providing again, and I had only been back in Michigan for a couple of weeks!

James and I met for dinner and I talked almost the whole two hours. There was so much to tell him. At one point I stopped, looked into his eyes and asked, "Why did you really want to meet with me?" (I started thinking that maybe he had cancer or something horrible.) His response was, "I just wanted a friend." Oh, OK! Then I started talking again. He called me again the day after and asked about the singles' get together. He came to the park, and we had a great time. Then he invited me to spend a day with him out at the lakeshore. That day changed everything!

James and I had been on the drama team together for about four years. We had learned a lot about each other during that time. I knew he was an honest, godly man. His character was impeccable. He was caring and encouraging. He was a prayer warrior. Our team would share prayer requests, and praying was always a part of our time together as a team. James was compassionate and often asked how I was doing with the migraines. He was also a great teacher. He brought out a talent that I had no idea was even in me.

Funny thing is—he felt the same way about me and my character. We knew we were both at the same level in our spiritual maturity. We seemed to talk about anything and everything. It was a glorious day out at Lake Michigan that day. We went to the beach, to lunch, did a little sightseeing and window shopping. It was when he took me back to my car that my heart leaped higher than it had in a long time. Our first kiss—Wow!!!

After that first date, it was time for me to move again. It would be my fifteenth move. Whew! But I was an expert by then. And this time would be so much easier. When I moved back to Michigan from Arizona, I only brought back what I could fit in my car. I left the furniture and household items for one of my teacher friends who was buying her first house. Anyway, I was moving from my son's apartment to stay with a friend closer to my new job. This friend allowed me to rent a room, and it would take me only thirty minutes to get to work instead of an hour. I was hired to be a supervisor in a retail optometrist office/store inside a mall. The job was working out well, and it was easy to be a supervisor there.

James and I started dating in June 2008, and we would often meet on Saturday mornings for breakfast. We would meet half-way at a small town family restaraunt. Then I would be off to work the afternoon/evening shift. It was one Saturday morning in August when I was on my way to meet him that I had to pull over and make a phone call. I felt that God had given me a prophecy. Once again I heard His small quiet voice speaking to my heart. And it was HUGE! I called my friend Joy and asked her to write something on her calendar. I wanted to remember the date that God gave me the message. And I wanted her to be a witness that on that day God told me that James and I would be getting married the following spring. I was elated. And ready to marry again. I wasn't sure if James was ready to marry again, so I did not say anything about the message from God until he proposed in December of that year. Then I had Joy verify that I knew in August. I just had to wait for him to know.

One thing I knew about James was that he would take good care of me. It was in the winter of 2008/2009 when I became really sick with the stomach flu and then a migraine on top of it. James was so gracious to drive an hour to pick me up from my house, drive another hour to take me to the hospital, and then a half hour to take me back to his house. I stayed at his house that night, and when I was well enough, he drove me the hour back to my house. That was four and a half hours of driving those two days to take care of me. What a guy!

In January we started making wedding plans. Just a small

wedding with our immediate families and a few friends. I wanted a real wedding this time with a real wedding dress, flowers, and decorations. I asked my daughter to stand up with me, and James asked his best friend to stand up with him. It was another glorious day in April 2009 with a clear blue sky, puffy white clouds and a warm spring breeze. We were married in a small chapel at the church where we had first met about thirteen years earlier. After the wedding, and since it would have taken me at least an hour to drive to work, I decided to quit my job and start substitute teaching in the school district where James lived. We were so in love, and it has only gotten better and better over the past eleven years! We could not be happier. Our relationship truly is the fairy tale that came true.

SEVEN

Cutting Her Out

I lose my way
And it's not too long before you point it out
I cannot cry
Because I know that's weakness in your eyes
I'm forced to fake
A smile, a laugh everyday of my life
My heart can't possibly break
When it wasn't even whole to start with
—*Because of You* by Kelly Clarkson

My stepfather, Jessie, had been having some health issues, and he just didn't feel well at our wedding. I wish James could have known him when he was well. He was a very kind and gentle Christian man. After the wedding he was in and out of the hospital several times. It was in September 2009 when he passed away. I got the call from Mom to come up to the hospital, because he was not expected to live through the day. I'm glad I took my Bible and was able to read some scripture to him before he passed. My son and my brother, with his family, were all there. After we had all said our goodbyes, we decided that Mom shouldn't be home alone that night. So Luke took her car to her house, and James and I brought Mom home to our house for the night.

In the morning she said, "Uh! That sofa was NOT comfortable! I'm never going to stay here again." (That was the thanks that we got for inviting her to stay the night with us. But it was typical Mom.) James made eggs, bacon and toast for breakfast, but she didn't even thank him. She just continued to complain about things at our house. She seemed to be in a big hurry to get back home, start making calls, and arranging the funeral. I tried to get her to relax, but she continued to rush me while I was getting ready to go to town. I had planned on staying with her for the day as she made arrangements. But she insisted I could go back home, and she would let me know when she would need me, probably the next day. I thought that was odd, but I acquiesced.

She called me later that day to tell me to be to her house first thing in the morning. She also explained that my cousin would be flying in from California for the funeral. I would need to pick her up from the airport. The next day we met with the funeral director and made the arrangements. We also discussed what she wanted for the luncheon after the funeral. We tossed around a few ideas, but she was determined to rent a nearby banquet hall and have them cater it. I told her that was a lot of money to spend. Why not just have her church ladies make food and take it to the hall across the street from the funeral home for next to nothing? Nope. And I thought she might actually listen to me for once. She was adamant, "This is what I want. And John can pay for half of the cost. It will be perfect." John was Jessie's only child, and he would be inheriting all of his dad's money. I had no clue how much he was inheriting, but I was sure John would not appreciate the bill. But I just kept my mouth shut and let her do whatever.

We went to the funeral home, the hall, the florist, etc. I took her home and would be returning the next day with my cousin in tow. My cousin would be staying with Mom for a few days to help console her.

Just before the funeral, Mom gave John the bill for the hall. He was NOT happy. He came unglued. I was afraid that would happen. I took my brother aside and told him about the hall expense. Luke then stepped in and calmed John down. Mom never has liked John, and he knew it. Mom doesn't like a lot of people.

After the luncheon, Luke and I joined Mom and my cousin at her house for an hour or so before it was time to go to the cemetery. Apparently, at the funeral, John had asked Luke to get his dad's wallet and his mother's Bible from our mom. John was not in any mood to talk to her. So while we were at Mom's, Luke asked for those items. Mom walked into the bedroom with Luke where she pulled out the wallet from a dresser drawer. Then she said she did not have the Bible.

At the cemetery the wallet was passed on. Then we all headed back home. We could all rest and deal with the grief in our own ways. The next morning when I woke up I had an urgent text from Luke. He said to call him asap. He had been awake all night and was very anxious. He said, "Remember yesterday when Mom and I went into the bedroom for the wallet?" I answered in the affirmative. He continued, "When Mom pulled it out of the drawer, she pulled out all of the money that was in there. She rolled it up into her hand and slipped it back into the drawer." I said, "Yeah. OK." Then Luke told me how the wad of money was so big she could hardly contain it all in her hand. He was upset because that much money should not have been in the wallet, and whatever was there should go to John. "But what denominations were they? Ones, twenties, or hundreds?" Luke had no clue. Mind you, Luke had worked in a bank for several years and knew what large sums of money looked like. I asked him what we should do. He didn't know, but we needed to try and find out how much was there. We kind of left it at that and went about our day.

I got ready and headed over to Mom's to pick up my cousin and take her back to the airport. While we were in the kitchen talking to Mom, my cousin and I heard what sounded like the front door open and a voice. I went over to see who was there. Nobody. Not a soul. I can assure you that the voice said, "Jessie?" My cousin and I just looked at each other and said, "What in the world...?" We had both heard the voice. Mom didn't, but her hearing is really bad. Mom said her goodbyes to my cousin, and we were off to the airport again.

When I left the airport I decided to call John and tell him what Luke saw the day before. Come to find out, he wasn't surprised. He had been to the bank to look at his dad's accounts. Apparently, Mom had been helping herself to Jessie's money in very large amounts over the past month or so. I believe she was going to the ATM on a daily basis and withdrawing the max amount. Since Jessie had been in and out of the hospital for a couple of months, that would definitely add up. I told John that Luke and I would do what we could to get to the bottom of it, and we would call him back. I called Luke and told him about what John said. He said to meet him at Mom's house in a half hour, and we would definitely get to the bottom of it. So I did.

Luke told Mom to get out all of her bank books, statements, etc. According to Mom, she was just making sure she had enough money to live on once Jessie was gone. My brother was not impressed. After we went through everything, we estimated that Mom needed to repay John at least $10,000. It was probably more, but we couldn't verify it.

Along with the conversation about money, Luke also brought up some other things that Mom had never taken responsibility for. (I let him do all of the talking because she never listens to me. I just kept nodding my head in agreement with what he was saying.) He told her that we really didn't trust her and haven't trusted her since that day back in 1980 when she was arrested in the grocery store. I emphatically agreed. It was the truth.

The other thing he brought up was the fact that Mom had always played favorites, and it had been very hurtful to me. Luke knew he was the favorite, and I was just a peon in my Mom's eyes. He asked her,"What if we were to play favorites between you and Dad? What if we never came to see you, but rather spent the time and every holiday with Dad? How would you feel?" She agreed that wouldn't be much fun for her. But she still did not understand what was wrong with playing favorites. She had a favorite aunt when she was growing up. She had her favorite sister and her favorite niece. Our meeting was fruitless. After two hours of trying to help Mom understand how she had done some things wrong, she still didn't get it. She never confessed to any wrongdoing. Ever. She has never made an apology either. To anyone.

Before we left her house that day, Luke told Mom to go to the bank the next morning and get a money order. He said, "Mom, You are the only one who knows how much you should give back to John. I hope you will think long and hard about how much to make that money order out for. We will be back here tomorrow at eleven am to pick it up and deliver it to John. Oh, and by the way, include with it anything else that should be given back to John. Like maybe his mother's Bible." We let John know the plan and would see him the next day.

The next day I met Luke at his office to ride with him. We stopped at Mom's and went in. She had a sealed envelope with the money order in it. She also had a whole box of stuff to go with it. Imagine that! There was the Bible, some photographs, and a few other items that John was sure to be happy to have. We left with the loot and started out on the one and a half hour drive to John's. We were both nervous not knowing how much money was in the envelope. We just hoped it would be at least what John was expecting.

When we arrived, John was very pleased to have the items. As for the money, Luke told him to wait until we left to open the envelope. We didn't want to know the amount. Luke said, "John, My sister and I have done all we can in regards to our mom and the money. If you are not satisfied with the amount, feel free to pursue further action. We get it, and we are sorry for all that has happened." We visited for a few minutes longer, and then Luke and I went back outside to his truck. I had turned my head to buckle my seatbelt when I heard, "He just gave us the thumbs up!" What? Luke said that John was in the doorway and was giving us the thumbs up that the amount was good. I looked up and was so pleased to see John smiling at us. Whew! That mess was over and done with. Luke and I were so thankful.

On the way back to our hometown, Luke and I talked about a lot of things including how we should go forward with relating to Mom. We were both feeling bad that she could not see her bad decisions as being wrong. We decided to let things calm down before we went to her again.

I had known what a narcissist was, but decided to do some research and see if I could better understand Mom's behavior. The first thing I did was go to my dictionary/thesaurus (New Oxford American Dictionary):

Narcissism, noun
extreme selfishness, with a grandiose view of one's own talents and a craving for admiration, as characterizing a personality type.

Narcissistic, adjective
vain, self-loving, self-admiring, self-absorbed, self-obsessed, conceited, self-centered, self-regarding, egotistic, egotistical, egoistic; full of oneself.

I found that people can have a mental illness called Narcissistic Personality Disorder (NPD.) What I found was that the symptoms of NPD can be similar to the traits of individuals with strong self-esteem and confidence. Narcissists have such an elevated sense of self-worth, that they value themselves as inherently better than others, when in reality they have a fragile self-esteem, cannot handle criticism, and will often try to compensate for this inner fragility by belittling or disparaging others in an attempt to validate their own self-worth. In order for a person to be diagnosed with NPD, they must meet five or more of the following symptoms:

- **Has a grandiose sense of self-importance** (exaggerates achievements and talents, expects to be recognized as superior without commensurate achievements)

- **Is preoccupied with fantasies of unlimited success, power, brilliance, beauty, or ideal love**
- **Believes that he or she is "special" and unique** and can only be understood by, or should associate with, other special or high-status people (or institutions)
- **Requires excessive admiration**
- **Has a very strong sense of entitlement** (unreasonable expectations of especially favorable treatment or automatic compliance with his or her expectations)
- **Is exploitative of others** (takes advantage of others to achieve his or her own ends)
- **Lacks empathy** (is unwilling to recognize or identify with the feelings and needs of others)
- **Is often envious of others** or believes that others are envious of him or her
- **Regularly shows arrogant, haughty behaviors or attitudes** (https://en.wikipedia.org/wiki/Narcissistic_personality_disorder)

This is absolutely my mom. It describes her to a "T." In my opinion, she meets most if not all of these nine symptoms! I also learned that narcissistic parents demand certain behavior from their children, because they see the children as extensions of themselves and need the children to represent them in the world in ways that meet the parent's emotional needs. This parenting "style" most often results in estranged relationships with the children, coupled with feelings of resentment and self-destructive tendencies. One problem with getting help for these individuals is that they believe there is nothing wrong with them, so why would they need help? In a sense, it would be like leading a horse to water, but no matter what, they won't drink.

Luke and I had several discussions about how we should

proceed with Mom. We went to her and tried to reason with her again. Two hours later she agreed that she would go with us to family counseling. Luke set up the appointment, and we met with a counselor the following week. One of the first things the counselor had us do was ask one another for forgiveness and to extend that forgiveness. I got to go first. Ugh! I told Mom I was sorry for any and all times that I did wrong to her or hurt her feelings. Would she forgive me? She said, "Yes." Then it was her turn. She asked me for forgiveness, but in the same breath, she said, "but I don't think I've done anything wrong." The counselor stopped her and told her that was not an option. "You need to ask forgiveness and then wait for an answer." In my mind I knew something was very wrong with my mom.

Then it was Luke's turn. But he looked toward the counselor and said, "No, I won't do it. Mom is just saying words that you tell her to say. Why should I say I forgive her when it won't mean anything?" The counselor said that was ok, and we would move on. We had several meetings before the counselor decided that a female counselor who was more versed in family dynamics might work out better for us. Nope. Didn't change a thing. And Mom actually went to her a couple of times on her own.

So here we were at the holiday time in 2009 wondering how to proceed. Luke and I decided to just let Mom be, and we would spend the holidays with our dad that year. In January Mom was so upset, and my brother asked her how she liked being the non-favorite parent? She didn't like it. Yet she never has changed.

After that I decided to interact with her as little as possible. I was tired of her putting me down, making me mad, and just being mean to me. At that time I came to realize how unhealthy it was to be afraid of getting a phone call or an email from my own mother. And worse yet, having her come to our house uninvited. She was known to pop in on occasion. Not necessarily a good thing to do to newlyweds. I decided not to answer her calls. I would let it go to voicemail and see why she was calling. If I felt the need, I would call her back. The anxiety inside of me was getting out of control. I would literally hold my breath and break out into a sweat whenever she did call or email. That went on for about a year. Then it happened.

One Monday evening in February 2011, I went to Bible study at the church like I did every Monday. I turned my phone off when I arrived and went about the study. When we were done, and I turned my phone back on, it was blowing up with phone calls and text messages. Several of them were from my brother. I didn't read the messages or listen to the voicemails; I just called him right away. Something must be really wrong. Maybe it was one of our parents.

He asked me if I had talked to a lady named Janet from Texas? I answered, "No. Who is Janet?" He wouldn't tell me the details but said I needed to call her right away. My curiosity was killing me. I called her even before I left the church. She answered and asked if I was Marsha's daughter? I answered, "Yes—"

After Jessie died, Mom had gone back to dating and was asked by her current boyfriend to go with him to Texas for several weeks. Not a bad offer when you live in Michigan and it is February! He had a sister there who worked on a ranch. She was going to let them stay with her and help out on the ranch. Sounded like a lot of fun, right?

Janet went on to tell me that she was the boyfriend's sister, but she wanted my mom out of her house immediately. She was not welcome to stay there any longer. Janet suspected my mom was stealing from her. Mom had been very mean to Janet, and she had had enough. Would I buy a plane ticket for her to fly home? I politely said, "Yep. That is my mom. But no, I will not buy her a plane ticket. She can figure it out herself. Mom has a credit card, and she knows how to use it. She has also made plenty of plane reservations in her day. I'm so sorry this has happened. I suggest that you tell her to pack her things and then drop her off at the airport. She'll figure out a way to get home." Janet was surprised (apparently Luke had refused to buy a ticket also) and told me, "You and your brother seem like the nicest people. I'm sorry you have such a rotten mom."

As you can imagine I was on fire when I left the church that night. I got home and told James all about the phone call. I was so done with her! And it was time for me to take control of my life and cut her out. I sat down and penned a letter. I probably even cursed a bit too. My letter was short and concise. I didn't want her to have any doubt about my decision. Here is the final product:

February 15, 2011
Mom,

Today I received a phone call from Janet in Rabbit River, Texas. That settled it for me—once and for all. I no longer have any doubts about what to do. You may have given birth to me, but you are no longer my "mom."

Luke and I have tried to help you through talking, counseling, etc., and you still do not understand. There is nothing else I can do to get you to understand. You have used me for the past forty-plus years to be your scapegoat and gopher, and I refuse to do it anymore. I will no longer allow you to use me or hurt me. I am not five years old and will not do what you tell me to do anymore.

What I can do at this point is protect myself. I am stepping out of your life for my own emotional and mental health. I will no longer allow you to consume so much of my time, thoughts, and energy. You will no longer be able to control or manipulate me. I ask that you do not call or email. If you do, I will not respond. You are also no longer welcome in our home. I am done playing your games and will no longer allow you to be a part of my life. Do not ask me or my husband for anything in the future. We will not respond.

I signed my name, left a note for James, and headed to her house at midnight. I felt a huge weight lifted off of me when I left the note and walked back out of her house. That was nine years ago. She did write me a note and sent it in the mail. I did not respond. Thankfully she never called or emailed in over nine years. I did go see her one time in the hospital because my cousin talked to her on the phone, and he thought she was dying. I wanted to see for myself. She was not dying. She claimed she had a stroke and some heart problems. But when my brother spoke with the medical staff, they told him that they could find no evidence of either. Cutting her out of my life was one of the best decisions I have ever made. I have felt so free from my mom that I could have said the following. (It is a quote from Jane Eyre in the book of the same name by Charlotte Bronte): "I am no bird; and no net ensnares me: I am a free human being with an independent will."

Remember the sleeping mamas in my dream, back in the Introduction? The young mama was my mom when she was a young woman and raising me. The reason she was asleep is that she is no longer a young woman. That part of her life is over. The old woman sleeping is my mom as an old woman. She is now in her eighties, but she is asleep because she no longer has a direct influence on my day to day life. The TV with Satan's voice is the struggles I still have. His voice still plays in my head sometimes, and it sounds just like my mom. Thankfully, as time goes along, the voices play less and less frequently.

EIGHT

My Health

For it has been granted to you on behalf of Christ not only to
believe on him, but also to suffer for him.
—Philippians 1:29

When James and I got married in 2009 I was feeling great. I
had turned forty the year before and was elated that throughout
my thirties I only had migraines once or twice a year. We were
married in April, and in June I started to feel not so good. I
couldn't really pinpoint why or how I was feeling, but it started
with abdominal pain, nausea, brain fog.—And as the days
progressed I was feeling worse and worse. By the end of the
month I went to the nurse practitioner, and she ordered some
blood-work. She got the results back and had me come in right
away. She was very concerned that I had high blood-sugar and
needed to take some medicine. She diagnosed me with type

two Diabetes and sent me home with five prescriptions. I was in shock and went home to tell James that I must be really sick, because I came home with five kinds of medicine to take everyday.

So began the next chapter of my life. Unfortunately, it all happened while we were still newlyweds. What we had planned did not happen. For reasons we have yet to discover, God had other plans for us. His plan included lots of different doctors, medical tests, surgeries, deep depression and anxiety. Once I started taking all of those medicines for the Diabetes, we thought I would start feeling better. Nope. I continued getting worse and worse. I was having trouble working a full day because I would be in pain and felt exhausted. I went back to see my doctor, and he ordered some more tests. One of the tests was a CT of my abdomen. The test showed that I had a gall stone. So I went to the surgeon, and we scheduled surgery to remove my gall bladder.

Two weeks after surgery I returned for my follow-up appointment. He asked me how I was feeling. I said, "I feel no different. Still have the pain and I'm still exhausted." He was sorry to hear that but said there was nothing more he could do for me. I needed to return to my family doctor. And then more tests. Finally I asked my family doctor to refer me to a gynecologist. When I went to see her, she of course ordered more tests. Nothing showed up on any of my tests. Everything came back normal. Since I was forty, and sure I would never have anymore children, I asked if she would do a hysterectomy. She finally agreed but was not sure it was the best idea.

In January 2010 I went into the operating room again. The doctor would use a scope to look around in my abdomen before she would decide to do the surgery laparoscopically, or if she would have to cut me open. After surgery I was in so much pain that I was screaming in the recovery room and all the way down the hall to my patient room. I had a morphine pump, but it wasn't touching the pain. My husband finally asked if they could give me a dose of Phenergan. That is one of my Migraine rescue meds that works fairly well. They finally tried that, and almost instantly I was feeling better and fell asleep. When I awoke, the doctor came in and told me that when she looked in my abdomen, it was full of endometriosis. It was all over my organs including the abdominal wall, ovaries and uterus. She took out the ovaries and uterus but had to scrape and cut away the rest. I was in pretty rough shape. At last we had an answer! Now I could heal and get back into life. Or so we thought.

Six weeks later I was still on the sofa unable to hardly move. I was battling an infection from the surgery, and I was getting more and more depressed. James had started doing the household chores, the grocery shopping, and the cooking. And he was still working full-time. When we went back to my family doctor, we were at our wits end. I had done my research and asked if he would refer me to The Mayo Clinic. He did that, and I was put on a waiting list. That's how they do things. We had no idea how long of a wait.

My incision finally healed, and I was able to get back into our bed. And there I stayed. I knew I was headed into another *Dark Night of the Soul.* For week after week and then month after month we waited. And I kept getting worse and worse. I had so little energy that when James took me to some places like the art museum or the botanical gardens, he would push me around in a wheelchair. Those outings were very few and far between, but he did his best to get me out of the house when I could muster the energy. I started calling Mayo Clinic once a week to see if there were any cancellations. Finally in June

2010 I got the call that they could see me the next week. Yes! We were finally going to get answers! Or were we?

We were told to expect to be there (Rochester, Minnesota) for up to two weeks depending on what they found. James took his two week vacation time to drive there. We made the drive in two days because I was too weak to sit in the car that long at one time. The first doctor that I saw was a doctor of internal medicine. He was the one who would line up all of the other doctors for me to see during my visit. He also started ordering the tests. The first thing we did was try to explain my journey. It was very hard for me because as soon as I would try to explain, I would start sobbing. Thankfully my incredible husband had documented everything. From every blood test, to my colonoscopy, to the surgeries, and every medicine I had tried. While I was trying to describe the abdominal pain, I said it felt like I was having a migraine, only the pain was in my belly not my head. He listened and took a lot of notes. Before we left his office, we had a plan. It was a twenty page plan. But it was a plan for the next several days. It included seeing all of the specialists that might be able to help. The first thing on the plan was to go to the lab and have my blood drawn for testing.

As I was laying on the table, James watched as they drew about thirty vials of blood from my vein. He was shocked. They tested for everything under the sun. Literally. Then I was off to my next appointment with the next doctor. I cannot even express all that we went through and how difficult it was on me.

After five days of intense testing and telling my story to doctor after doctor, we had not learned anything. We were still in the dark as to what was wrong with me. I had another endoscopy, an MRI, a stress test, pulmonary testing; I was poked and prodded so many times I lost count. I was given cortisone shots, electrical zap treatment, and on and on and on. With every doctor I saw, I would tell them about my migraines and say, "It feels like I have a migraine only the pain is in my belly. And I am so depressed. Please help me." I begged. I pleaded. But no answers.

When we went back to our tiny hotel room at the end of Friday, we knew we were in for a long weekend. Monday was the fourth of July, and the clinic was not open. Everywhere we went James pushed me in a wheelchair. He tried to get me outside as much as possible for fresh air. We ended up having to do some laundry at the hotel, because we had only brought enough clothing for a week. We had to eat out for every meal. I had not been eating much because I had nausea all of the time. And it was so difficult for me to think that it literally took me forty-five minutes of looking over the menus before deciding what I wanted to order. Much of the time the only thing I could do was cry.

On Tuesday we started seeing doctors again. With each new doctor we were back to square one. Every test I had while at the clinic came back normal. Every treatment they tried on me did not work. Every doctor just passed me off to the next one. Until Thursday of the second week. I was meeting with a neurologist. She wanted another MRI of my upper vertebrae. After the procedure we went back to her for her findings. Nothing. She asked if I was scheduled to see a psychiatrist? I was—a month from then. We told her there was no way we could make the trip back in a month. She pulled some strings and got me an appointment on Friday.

On Friday I went for psychological testing and then saw the doctor for the results. Once again, repeating my story for the hundredth time... This doctor asked if I was on an anti-depressant. I told her no, that none of the doctors would prescribe it for me. She wanted to admit me to the psychiatric hospital, but we told her we had to leave the next day for home. James had to be back to work on Monday. She was willing to write me a prescription to get filled that day, but I had to promise her I would get into a psychiatrist as soon as I was home. We agreed.

On Saturday James drove all the way through to home. When we got here, we both collapsed into bed. On Sunday I woke up and could not get out of bed. I was hardly able to move my body. I told James two things: "Get all of the pain meds out of this house, because I'm about to take them all and be done with it. And call my counselor who used to work at the psychiatric hospital. She will know what to do."

James got the meds out of the house. He called the counselor and explained the situation. She wanted to know if I could wait until morning to get help. I didn't know. I couldn't make any decision at that point. She talked with me and asked if I was willing for James to make that decision for me? I said, "Yes, of course." So he made one of the hardest decisions of his life. He packed a bag for me, and we headed to the hospital.

It was late by the time we got all checked in, and I had to say goodbye to my husband. I held him so tight and didn't want to let go. He assured me that I would be ok, and he would be back to see me the next day. When he left me there, I was sure that I would never see this man again. Why would he come back? We had only been married a little over a year, and I had done nothing but be sick. I went to my assigned room and cried and cried and cried. It was my darkest night ever. I hope to my Lord I will never be in that place again. I wanted to kill myself, but there was no way I could while in that hospital.

The next afternoon I was sitting in the commons area when James walked in. He had brought me gifts. You cannot even imagine how happy I was that he came back. I didn't understand why, but I hugged him so tight I thought he might burst.

I ended up staying in that hospital for two weeks. When I was admitted I had an ice bag that I kept on my belly all of the time. It numbed the pain so I could at least tolerate it. By the time I was ready to go home, I had been on the mental health meds for long enough that my mood was getting much better. And my abdominal pain was easing up a bit.

A few years after that hospital stay I was feeling better, but the pain was still there. It would come and go and move from side to side. Then I got some information about a twelve-year-old family member. Due to her recent abdominal pain and vomiting, she was diagnosed with "Abdominal Migraines" at the local children's hospital. When her mother first said this term in our conversation, I was in shock. I had never heard the term and was very intrigued. I quickly looked it up on WebMD and was blown away by what I read. For the past four and a half years James and I had been searching for answers. For those years I had told every doctor I had seen that it felt like I had a migraine—only the pain was in my abdomen. Test after test, surgery after surgery, procedure after procedure, treatment after treatment—and still the pain kept returning.

Throughout the month of March 2014 I was once again "taken down" by this pain. Once again I went to my doctor. Once again I had x-rays. Again was sent to a specialist who ordered more tests. Again the tests all read "normal." We were so frustrated—again. Finally after three weeks of messing around with the doctors, the tests, and the pain—finally I decided, "Hmmm, I am going to take my migraine medicine. Let's see if this helps." Ya know what? It helped! The pain went away, I slept for a couple of days and was gaining my strength back again. My appetite was back. My pain was gone. I was finally feeling better! I had a diagnosis, and I now knew (without a shadow of a doubt) what was wrong with me. I have had migraines in my head since I was an infant. Now I knew that it was the same problem—just in my abdomen. I now knew how to treat it. I now knew the answer. I was getting better finally. Or at least we thought I was.

At this point my migraine headaches had become more and more frequent. The next two years found me in bed again nearly every day of every month. My migraine meds were not working anymore. I would go to the ER for a treatment and get relief for a few hours. Then the pain was back. My neurologist decided to send me to another neurologist who specializes in Migraine. He only treats migraine patients. Once again I had to tell my story.

NINE

Today

"For I know the plans I have for you," declares
the Lord, "plans to prosper you
and not to harm you, plans to give you hope and a future."
—Jeremiah 29:11

My new neurologist, Dr. Applewood, has been a true godsend. He is the best doctor I have ever had. He does not treat the disease; he treats the patient. We had a treatment plan. I was trying new medications. I now go to his infusion center for treatment when my home meds do not cut through the pain. And I have gone in for inpatient treatments for seven days at a time when needed. I am happy to report that the migraines are better now.

I'm also happy to report that life in and of itself has calmed down. Both of my children are now adults with families of their own. They both have successful careers, and I could not be more proud of them. They have always amazed me. Oftentimes I have felt like I failed them, but alas, they both turned out real good. My kids, my brother and his family, and James's family all live in West Michigan where I am. I love being so close to my family. There is no way I could have stayed in Arizona.

James and I live in a beautiful house along the countryside of our small farming community. We also attend an incredible church that is only one mile from our home. Throughout all of my illnesses, we have had church members stepping up to the plate and being the church as Christ intended. People have brought in food when we needed it, and several of the ladies have taken me to my doctor appointments when James was at work. And then there are the prayers. Since day one of us being a part of this church, the congregation has been praying over me and for me. We are blessed!

The Old Testament book of Song of Songs is one of the greatest love stories ever told. It is truly incredible the way the husband and wife are so enamored with one another. It is refreshing in this day and age to have an account of the true meaning of marriage. This relationship is an example of what God intended for married couples.

The thing is, I can very truthfully say that Song of Songs is also the love story of James and me. Our time together has not been all sunshine and roses. Very far from it. Our marriage started off with the death of my stepfather, my poor health, the disowning of my mom, the darkest night of my soul, and now a young family member with cancer. But through it all, we have grown more and more in love each day. We are stronger together, and our love is sweeter each new day. James encourages my crazy creative ideas and is always ready to lend a hand.

The other day I read about a mother who gave her daughter some advice. She said to replace the word "love" in the love chapter (I Corinthians 13) with your man's name. If what you read is not accurate, he is not the one for you. I think this is incredible advice. So I decided to do that with James's name. Here is how it reads:

> "(James) is patient, (James) is kind. (He) does not envy, (he) does not boast, (he) is not proud. (James) is not rude, (he) is not self-seeking, (he) is not easily angered, (he) keeps no record of wrongs. (James) does not delight in evil but rejoices with the truth. (He) always protects, always trusts, always hopes, always perseveres." (I Corinthians 13: 4-7)

I can honestly say that this is a very accurate description of my husband. And I'm the most blessed woman alive.

As I sit down to complete this chapter, it is now June 2020. I had really been struggling with my depression when I got a phone call one evening about three months ago. It was my brother. He sounded upset and said that I needed to get to the emergency room asap. Mom had fallen, and she was in the ER not expected to live very long.

When James and I arrived at the ER, we learned that Mom had hit her head when she fell and had a severe brain bleed. There was nothing the doctors could do for her. The ER doctor told us that she could live a couple of hours or a couple of days. He was not sure. He told us that she could not hear out of her left ear or move her left limbs. Summer came to the hospital that night, and we all gave Mom our love and said our good-byes.

By the time we all left the hospital that night, Mom was

resting well in a regular room. She was on comfort care and well taken care of. The next few days were touch and go. Luke was spending most of his time at the hospital, and I would go relieve him for a few hours each day. It was really strange because one day Mom would be completely out of it and sleeping all day. Then the next day she was awake, watching TV, and talking with us. She knew what day it was, where she was at, and what was going on. One day when I was there I helped her eat a bowl of macaroni and cheese as well as a pudding cup. She asked me, "What flavor is the pudding?" I told her it was vanilla. She said it tasted just like her mother's homemade ice cream.

That first week of her being in the hospital was a rollercoaster. Luke and I kept waiting for the call saying that she was gone. My son and one of the other five grandchildren came to see her. They both gave her their love and said their good-byes. Mom knew that she was dying and said that she was ready. She was looking forward to seeing her sisters and a brother who were all in Heaven already. After that first week, the hospital said she needed to be moved to a nursing home. They could not keep her any longer.

Luke made arrangements for her to be transferred to one of the nursing homes across town and to get Hospice care. The problem was that our governor had just ordered a state-wide lockdown due to the Coronavirus pandemic. When Mom arrived at the nursing home, she would not be able to have any visitors whatsoever.

Luke was in contact with the nursing home and would get daily updates. She had been there for a week when he got the call one evening. She had passed. Exactly two weeks from the day she fell. We had already made all of the arrangements at the funeral home, so it was just a phone call to let them know. Two days later we had a graveside service. Due to the COVID-19 pandemic, we were not allowed to have a funeral with a lot of people. Luke and I were fine with that. We just wanted it to be over and done with. There were nine of us at the cemetery, including the funeral director.

Over the previous two weeks I had watched how several family members had been moved to tears watching my mom die. I, on the other hand, had no emotion. No feelings. I figured that was because of my depression, but it was a bit concerning. I've been talking with my therapist about it, and we have concluded that I grieved the loss of my mother years ago. It had been nine years since we had a relationship. I think it is sad that she lived her last years without contact with most of her family. My son had no relationship with her; my daughter rarely spent any time with her; my brother had very little contact with her; and three of her other four grandchildren had no relationship with her. Her passing was truly a bittersweet event. Luke and I felt a sort of relief that she would no longer be able to torment our family.

A few years ago I learned that Mom had put my name, along with Luke's, on the deed to her home. That was the only thing she owned at the time of her passing. Mom was always saying that she had no money and even had to refinance her home a couple of times. So it was a pleasant surprise when we learned that she actually had some equity in her home. Luke and I got it ready to sell and found a buyer right away. This would be the last step in finding closure with regard to our mom.

As I contemplated my life, and the role my mother had played, I realized that the very last thing she did for me was a positive. With the sale of her home, she left me a nice amount of money that I was in no way expecting. I really was surprised that there would be any money left after paying the funeral home, hospital, and nursing home. Today I am thankful that the last thing my mom did for me was nice. Even though greed ruled much of her life, in her dying she gave Luke and me each a nice amount of money. I in turn was able to do something nice for my children. I am so happy that I was able to bless my own kids with some money for the first time in my life. Thank you, Mom.

PART II

Lessons Learned

TEN

What is Migraine Disease?

Only in faith can you endure your worst nightmare and yet
dare to dream of a God who hears your cries.
—Reverend David Feddes

I have already explained a little bit about the disease but want
to go into some more detail so you can try and understand
what I go through. Let's start with Google: "Migraine Disease
is a neurological, and oftentimes hereditary disease. Migraine
is typically characterized by severe, recurring head pain,
usually located on one side of the head and one or more of
the following associated symptoms: nausea, vomiting, and
increased sensitivity to light, sound, and smell."

Ok, so it is just a really bad headache, right? Wrong! The
migraine pain has always been the same for me. It is always
located on the left side of my head, neck and shoulder. It is a

constant stabbing pain and feels like a dagger is burrowed right through the middle of my left eye. At the same time, it feels like a constant bolt of lightening is striking through the top of my head on the left side. Finally, there is pain radiating from my left shoulder and neck up into the back of my head. As well as the sharp pain, there are also the following symptoms that accompany a migraine attack: severe nausea and vomiting, light and sound sensitivity, extreme fatigue, brain fog, excessive yawning, clinical depression and anxiety. When I have a migraine attack (which can last for days at a time), the only way to cope is to take my medications and hide away in my bedroom with black-out curtains and a completely silent house. Sometimes the attack will wake me from a sound sleep in the middle of the night at three or four am. I wake up screaming for my husband to get me some medicine. It may seem weird, but sometimes I feel like beating my head against the wall to relieve the pain. At other times the attack will come on slowly over the course of a few hours or days. I constantly live with the fear of when the next one will strike.

Migraine has stolen an untold number of weeks and months from my life—maybe even years. I am unable to work outside the home. Oftentimes I am unable to go to family or social events. When I am able, it drains me completely, and I have to come home and sleep for several hours to recover. It is a successful day when I'm able to attend an event without it causing a migraine attack. Sometimes I am unable to do everyday chores like grocery shopping and laundry. And then my husband does all of that for me.

I would love to be able to work full-time and enjoy my family, friends, church services, Bible studies, etc. I also want to be able to go bike riding, swimming, and hiking. I would love to host holidays in my home and have a backyard BBQ again.

We have spent thousands of dollars on countless non-traditional treatments including acupuncture, manual manipulation, vitamins, herbs, etc. without success. Also without success are all of the different oral medications, injectable medications, nerve block treatments, and IV treatments. Currently I manage with Botox treatments.

There are also some residual effects from having Migraine Disease: While trying the nerve block treatments, I ended up with worsening Diabetes. Now I am bound to taking insulin several times every day. I am also overweight. If I could just get up, get out, and get going—I could exercise, move around more, and hopefully lose weight. All of which would help the Diabetes and the migraines. There are times when I spend much of my time simply eating and sleeping. One goal with Migraine treatments is to help me sleep. That allows my body to relax and the medicines to do their work.

Have you ever been inside your house at night, all warm and snuggly, and watched a storm rage outside? From the security inside, you admire the storm's raw beauty and the awesome energy being released. You discuss the meteorological implications or the fact that it might be delaying the ballgame. Or maybe just console yourself as you realize that you're glad you don't have to be out "on a night like this."

Now imagine you are out in that storm. Caught unaware and ill prepared, you are not faring well. Lightening flashes with blinding stabs, leaving you barely time to comprehend the images momentarily exposed, before you are once again plunged into darkness. Thunder, so loud and close, that even though you try to brace for its inevitable explosion, you are still involuntarily jolted each time it reports. You are wet to the bone, cold, shivering, lonely and scared. In fact, you are scared to death. If you could close your eyes and shut it all out, you would. But you cannot. You can only endure, minute by minute, each flash and each crash a thing to be painfully endured until the storm, in its own time, finally spends itself out.

Remember the paragraph that I wrote when I was sixteen? The storm is Migraine and the world is me.

When I was in college I took that paragraph and formed it into a poem:

THE STORM

My day is sunny and bright
and without warning, without a sign,
the ***lightning strikes***, and the storm begins.
That constant bolt – piercing deep
down
  through
    the
      top
        of
          my
            head.

It penetrates
the entire
left side
of my
body.

For hours.................................and then days,
the   piercing   pain   relentlessly   pursues   my   life.
When the storm finally seems to let up –
the lightning less intense,
that's when the next stage
of the storm begins.
The lightning ceases and the **heavy**
rains
pour
down.
As the flood waters rise, I struggle to keep from drowning
in my depression.
Just when I am about to
give up,

the sun peaks through the ominous clouds
with a hint of hope.
THE SUN BREAKS THROUGH:

My Hope is Renewed.

Gradually the rain stops,
the flood waters dry up,
and once again my days
become sunny and bright.

Soon after writing *The Storm* poem, I wrote the following:

Grace Rockwell

A HINT OF HOPE
(Sequel to *The Storm*)

This morning when I awoke,
I knew the Storm was still raging.

As I fought off the flood waters,
I willed my body to get out of bed.

Inch by inch, each limb moved methodically
and brought me closer to a vertical position.

After throwing back the covers,
I headed toward the kitchen for a drink.

On my way past the table,
a small scrap of paper caught my eye.

I saw: *Dear Mom,*
and plopped down on the couch to read the rest:

 I hope you get better today. O.k.
If you need us just call the school.
We are good. I love you a lot.
You are my sunshine.

And at that moment,
the flood waters began to retreat.

ELEVEN

Created by God

For you created my inmost being;
you knit me together in my mother's womb.
I praise you because I am fearfully and wonderfully made;
your works are wonderful,
I know that full well.
My frame was not hidden from you
when I was made in the secret place,
when I was woven together in the depths of the earth.
Your eyes saw my unformed body;
all the days ordained for me were written in your book
before one of them came to be.
—Psalm 139: 13–16

As a teacher, I know God created me to help others understand stuff. Stuff like reading, math, life-skills; but most important by far, to help them understand who God is, what the Bible is all about, and why Jesus Christ is our only hope. I also believe that my story (my own life experiences and journey) will help others learn how to completely embrace a relationship with Christ and grow in their relationship with Him.

I believe that God sent me to college (from 1996–2002) for "such a time as this." He has a plan to put my education to work for Him. And in His time, He will lead me to the next step. He knows my heart, my mind, my strengths, my weaknesses, my desires, my abilities, and my gifts. I know this without a doubt, because He gave them to me.

I also believe that God has a purpose for every experience and all of the suffering I have endured. It has been through those times that I have clung onto Him for my very life. I love this quote by Holley Gerth: "In the place between what is comfortable and what seems like it will surely kill us is often where we become all we were created to be." Through it all God is growing me into the woman he wants me to be. I do not say this lightly. For those of you who are suffering now, please hold on. God does have a plan for you. He will use it for good. Please trust me on this one.

I have always loved learning. That's just how God created me. Not just book learning, but learning from life and from other people too. Did you know that we learn from every experience we have and every person we meet? And others are learning from us. Think about a coworker or friend. Think about how they live day to day. What is their character like? Do you agree, disagree with their lifestyle, or have an opinion about them? Of course you do. We all do. Maybe that person is kind, generous, and caring. You look up to and respect them. You are learning what makes a person kind, generous, and caring. On the other hand, maybe that coworker or former friend has stabbed you in the back or talked down to you. From them you have learned, and hopefully it will influence you the next time you start to gossip or say negative things to a person.

Over the years I have watched people, listened to, and learned from them. From my mom I learned how not to raise children. I learned that people should be nice to each other. On the other hand, I've also watched godly people and seen what they do and what they say. I want to learn from them also. I like how Gary Thomas does this. In his book *Seeking the Face of God* he writes, "When I see people who seem to have an unusual presence of Christ in their lives, I ask them questions. I want to know how they've become what they've become." (47) We all learn from one another. One time I heard that people come into our lives either for a reason, a season, or a lifetime. And we have a choice to make. Will we learn to say and do negative things or positive things in those relationships?

As for our experiences, the point here is not about what happens to you. It's about what you do with what happens to you. I learned this from a master teacher I used to work with. As for the difficult and stormy circumstances, we will not be the same person when we come out of it. Pain changes people. These are learning opportunities, and that's what the storms are all about. I've heard many times over the years that we can come out of those times either bitter or better. I decided a long time ago that life is too short to be bitter. I want to be better. Winston Churchill once said, "Personally I'm always ready to learn, although I do not always like to be taught." It's not always easy, but it is a matter of choice. Will your life lessons make you bitter or better?

Beginning on page thirty-five of *The Dark Night of the Soul*, John of the Cross explains that although the road is "so straight, dark and terrible," the soul's "conquests are incomparably greater." From here he goes into great detail about how our soul benefits from the journey in about twenty different ways. He wraps up this list of benefits on pages forty-four and forty-five by saying, "In this dark and arid night, this blessed soul grows in the fear of God...her longing to serve God alone remains fixed, stubborn and naked, which is a thing most pleasing to His sight. The afflicted spirit is a sacrifice to God. As the soul, therefore, knows that in this arid purgation where through she has passed, she has derived and acquired such precious gifts... the harmony of the senses and interior powers ceasing from their discursive motions and mental operations...they cannot hinder this spiritual freedom, and the house is left in silence and at peace."

As I keep coming back to these words, I am reminded that God has a purpose and divine plan for my life. Each day that finds me in bed without physical strength or mental capacity, I keep coming back to "touch home" and trust God for my future. It is a very dark road, but I know there is a glorious light at the end. Romans 8:28 tells us that "in all things God works for the good of those who love Him." Just like with Joseph in the Old Testament, we can say, "You intended to harm me, but God intended it for good to accomplish what is now being done." (Gen. 50:20) If you don't know the story, Joseph was the youngest of his brothers. He was the spoiled one and his brothers hated him. One day they sold him into slavery and told their father that Joseph had been killed by some ferocious animal. Years later the brothers were having a famine and went to the nearby city where Joseph had come into high power. They asked him for food and Joseph shared with them. Just like us, Joseph had a choice to either become bitter or better. He chose to forgive his brothers and become a better person.

When I think about the mean things my mom and Roger

said and did to me, I remember asking God, "Why? What did I do wrong?" Looking back, I now know that God used those circumstances for my good. I wouldn't be the person I am today if those things had not happened.

From a very early age I felt that God was with me. It was easy for me to trust Him and put my faith in Him at the age of eleven. It was the best thing I ever did. It was at the age of seventeen when I started really studying the Bible and growing my relationship with Christ. Oswald Chambers once wrote, "Living a life of faith means never knowing where you are being led. It is literally a life of faith, not of understanding and reason—a life of knowing Him who calls us to go." Once again it was a choice I made. I could have walked away from God and done life on my own. But I'm so glad I chose to live by faith.

As I was learning and seeking God, He continued to speak to me through the Bible, prayer and meditation. I learned that as a Christian, my identity should rest on Christ alone. I learned that at the cross Jesus took our sin and filth and gave us His righteousness. He gives it to us, but it is up to us to receive and accept it or not. His righteousness is perfect, clean, and beautiful. Ladies, we need to stop being so negative about ourselves and start looking at ourselves from God's point of view. He is the King and we are his daughters—His princess warriors. The enemy wants us to believe the lies and not stand up against the horrific things that so many women around the world endure.

I am so sick of hearing women complain that they are too fat, too stupid, too weak—No! In Christ we are beautiful. We are smart. We have power and dignity. Only when we start taking care of ourselves and loving ourselves, can we care for and love others.

I also believe it is very difficult for men to understand the conflicting feelings, ideas, and thoughts that women battle on a daily basis. It is not easy, as women, to see ourselves as designed in God's image. So many of the "images" of God are masculine. But since He created us in His image, men and women together are the perfect image of God. Male and Female. Masculine and Feminine. Not one or the other is more important. Not one or the other should dominate the other. We are all His children, and I would like to see more women come to understand this. I have learned that when we understand and embrace this truth—then we can be truly free. Free to be all that God wants us to be. So—on your darkest days, when you feel inadequate, unloved, and unworthy, "remember whose daughter you are and straighten your crown."

Along with becoming God's daughter, I also became His bride the day I accepted Jesus into my heart. Throughout the Bible God refers to us as His bride, and He compares it to our earthly marital relationships. He says that men and women "should leave their parents to be united and become one flesh. So they are no longer two, but one." Ephesians 5:31. This is certainly a great mystery that is hard to understand. But then when we apply the same premise to our relationship to God, it is even harder to fathom. It took a long time, but in 2006 I finally understood what this meant. I am the bride of Christ. The two shall become one. Not only do I desire to see God, and to experience Him, I get to be united with Him. I get to swim for the rest of eternity in the ocean of His love and never become tired, weary, or out of breath.

TWELVE

The Power of Forgiveness

For if you forgive men when they sin against you, your
heavenly Father will also forgive you. But if you do not
forgive men their sins, your Father will not forgive your sins.
—Matthew 6:14-15

Just like we have the choice of how we react to difficult
circumstances, we also have the choice of how we react to
others who sin against us. We can get angry and hold a grudge,
or we can forgive them. Jesus tells us in the book of Matthew
that if we choose to forgive, then God will forgive us. And in
Colossians 3:13, Paul tells the people, "Bear with each other
and forgive whatever grievances you may have against one
another. Forgive as the Lord forgave you."

Forgiving others is a choice, not a feeling. Forgiveness frees
us from resentment and prolonged anger. We choose not to

retaliate. Ephesians 4:31-32 tells us to "Get rid of all bitterness, rage and anger, brawling and slander, along with every form of malice. Be kind and compassionate to one another, forgiving each other, just as in Christ God forgave you." God tells us to forgive; it's the right thing to do. But the angry feelings won't go away immediately. Our choice to forgive is like the choice we make to turn off a fan. We can flip the switch, but the fan blades won't stop immediately. The blades slow down gradually and eventually come to a stop. The same is true when we are hurt by someone, and the blades of anger are spinning rapidly. We choose to flip the switch to forgiveness. The anger doesn't go away instantly, but the anger will lessen until one day we realize those feelings are gone. I have chosen to forgive numerous people throughout my life. A few of those people were ones I told you about in Part I. I was able to write those stories without having the angry negative feelings. The feelings of anger and resentment went away years ago.

Don't get me wrong, forgiving doesn't mean forgetting. Forgiveness means releasing the anger and tension you have toward someone who has hurt you. You can forgive someone and still keep them out of your life. Jim Smoke explains this well in his book *Growing Through Divorce*, "I have listened to many people tell me that they can forgive but they will never forget. And I would agree that on their own strength forgetting will be hard, if not impossible. I believe that the forgetting of things must be left up to God. We all know that time is a healer and time causes us to forget. As tensions and hurts are erased through seeking forgiveness, I believe we slowly forget the bad things and remember the good. You can always take personal action in the forgiveness realm. You will have to trust God and time with the forgetting area." (95) Smoke also assures us to

"Be aware that forgiveness is not an instant happening but a process that we grow into." (93)

People are often unreasonable, illogical, and self-centered. Forgive them anyway. I have learned that God is the only one who can love me perfectly and without fail. My family and friends will all fail me. I need to let go of looking for unfailing love from people because it can't happen. Take for instance my mom and how she has treated me over the past fifty years. As I was doing some research, I came across the definition of Attachment Disorders: "The psychological result of negative experiences with caregivers, usually since infancy, that disrupt the exclusive and unique relationship between children and their primary caregiver(s)." One researcher claims that "children in orphanages were prone to physical illness and had decreased appetites. They exhibited some stereotyped movements, self-stimulation, and an empty look in the eyes. They lacked normal responses of interest when people came close. They cried vaguely or softly many times a day and seemed unhappy. Many of these children seemed depressed and unresponsive to initiatives for interaction, as if resigned to affective deprivation."

I don't claim that I have an Attachment Disorder necessarily, but these descriptions seem to fit my behaviors and illnesses as an infant and young child. Ultimately, whether I have a disorder or not, I do have the choice to forgive my mom or not. In his book *Keys to a Deeper Life,* AW Tozer claims that "All offenses against God, against ourselves, against humanity, against human life—all offenses will be either forgiven or avenged." (71) You and I have the choice to forgive or to avenge. And if I remember correctly from my early church learning, God alone is the judge. But it takes humility to believe and live this. Thomas a Kempis explains that, "The more humble a man is in himself and the more obedient he is to God, the more wise and peaceful will he be in everything he will have to do." (37, *The Imitation of Christ*) I don't know about you, but I prefer to be wise and peaceful as opposed to the alternative.

I have come to believe that God is the judge, and He alone knows everyone so intimately that He can see what is in our hearts. He knows our motives. And not one of us can know absolutely everything about another person. Gary L Thomas explains this in *Seeking the Face of God:* "If others had had our advantages, they might have been much more faithful than we have been. If we had had their disadvantages, we might have done much worse. We simply don't know, and therefore we are incapable of accurately judging anyone." (140) You and I have the choice to be unforgiving which will lead to bitterness and a continual state of distress. Or we can choose forgiveness which will make us better and we will live in peace.

In Luke 6:27, Jesus tells us that we are to love our enemies. We should always treat others with love and mercy. Tozer tells us that we cannot fight sin with sin. He states, "Always it is more important that we retain a right spirit toward others than that we bring them to our way of thinking, even if our way is right. Satan has achieved a real victory when he succeeds in getting us to react in an unspiritual way toward sins and failures in our brethren. We cannot fight sin with sin or draw men to God by frowning at them in fleshly anger." (72)

You may wonder what you should do when people hurt you over and over again. How many times should we forgive someone? In Matthew 18:21-22, Jesus answers that very question: "Lord, how many times shall I forgive my brother when he sins against me? Up to seven times? Jesus answered, 'I tell you, not seven times, but seventy-seven times.'" Some Bible versions say seventy times seven. Either way, it is a lot.

Sometimes it is a daily battle. When those feelings of rage rear up, we need to forgive all over again whether it is every day or every hour. And no matter how many times a person hurts us, we are always to forgive them. But what if they are not sorry for what they did? What if they don't ever apologize? When Jesus was suffering on the cross, he addressed God, His Father even as he was being tortured by evil men. Those men were not sorry for what they were doing. They were doing anything but apologizing. Here is Jesus's response in Luke 23:34: "Jesus said, 'Father, forgive them, for they do not know what they are doing.'"

When we forgive others, God will forgive us. Because God forgives us, we are to forgive others. Forgiveness is not a feeling; it is a choice. Forgiving does not mean forgetting. Only God can love us perfectly; everyone else will fail. God alone knows us and our motives intimately. No matter how many times a person sins against us, we are to forgive them, even if they are not sorry and don't apologize. I hope you will choose to live a life of forgiveness.

THIRTEEN

The Power of Saying, "I'm Sorry."

Therefore I despise myself and repent in dust and ashes.
—Job 42:6

One of my Old Testament heroes is Job. The book of Job starts out by introducing Job as a blameless, upright man who feared God and shunned evil. Job had seven sons and three daughters. He owned thousands upon thousands of animals and a large number of servants. The book goes on to explain how Satan accused God of putting a hedge around Job and that is why he was blameless and upright. God disagreed with Satan and allowed him to destroy everything Job had, including his family, his animals, and even his health. Job replied to the devastation with, "Shall we accept good from God and not trouble?" Job did not sin through all of his adversities.

Although he did not sin, Job did struggle with depression. His lament can be understood in the following passages. (You may have said these very things at times. I know I have.):

> "May the day of my birth perish, and the night it was said, 'a boy is born!'...Why did I not perish at birth, and die as I came from the womb?... Why is light given to those in misery, and life to the bitter of soul, to those who long for death that does not come....I have no peace, no quietness; I have no rest, but only turmoil." Job 3:3-26

> "Oh, that I might have my request, that God would grant what I hope for, that God would be willing to crush me, to let loose his hand and cut me off!...What strength do I have, that I should still hope? What prospects, that I should be patient?" Job 6:8-11

> "Therefore I will not keep silent; I will speak out in the anguish of my spirit, I will complain in the bitterness of my soul." Job 7:11

Maybe like Job you have had friends try to help you through the hard times or when you are depressed. Unfortunately Job's friends were no help at all. What they did do was accuse him of wrongdoing. They told him that he was experiencing all of these hardships because he was plowing evil and sowing trouble. They told him that God was punishing him for his wickedness, that he was an evil man, and he did not know

God. Job knew that those were lies, and he called them out on it. Satan used these friends to try and get Job to believe these things and take on false guilt. Maybe you have been told that things have happened to you because you brought them on yourself. But you alone know the truth. Please do not take on false guilt. It is a lie from the enemy. Don't believe those voices that tell you, "You are not good enough." Remember my dream and how Satan came on the TV to tell me the lies? He wanted me to believe I was not good enough, I should not even try, and I should give up. Those lies are what Satan uses to make us feel horrible about ourselves and take on false guilt. If someone in your life is doing this to you, you do not need to apologize. You have done nothing wrong. Instead of believing them, call them out on it. If they won't listen, then distance yourself from them. They are not good for you. Sometimes I still hear the voice of my mom in the back of my head. I hear things like, "You can't do it." "You are terrible at that." and "You aren't good enough." At those times I speak out against the voices and say, "No! That is a lie, and I will not believe it."

Through it all, Job stayed humble. Humility is the first step to saying, "I'm sorry." Job tells God, "tell me what charges you have against me. If I am guilty—woe to me." Job pleads for God to show him the reasons for his plight, "But where can wisdom be found? Where does understanding dwell? Man does not comprehend its worth; it cannot be found in the land of the living. The deep says, 'It is not in me'; the sea says, 'It is not with me.' It cannot be bought with the finest gold, nor can its price be weighed in silver." (Job 28:12-15) Then in chapter thirty-two comes a friend who speaks to Job in love. This is part of Elihu's speech:

"But you have said in my hearing—I heard the very words—'I am pure and without sin; I am clean and free from guilt. Yet God has found fault with me; he considers me his enemy. He fastens my feet in shackles; he keeps close watch on all my paths.' But I tell you, in this you are not right, for God is greater than man...In a dream, in a vision of the night, when deep sleep falls on men as they slumber in their beds, he may speak in their ears and terrify them with warnings, to turn man from wrongdoing and keep him from pride, to preserve his soul from the pit, his life from perishing by the sword."
Job 33:8-18

Elihu continues with, "But those who suffer he delivers in their suffering; he speaks to them in their affliction." Finally, in chapters forty and forty-one, God speaks to Job:

"The Lord said to Job, 'Will the one who contends with the Almighty correct him? Let him who accuses God answer him!...Would you discredit my justice? Would you condemn me to justify yourself? Do you have an arm like God's, and can your voice thunder like his?'"
Job 40:1-9 "'Who then is able to stand against me? Who has a claim against me that I must pay? Everything under heaven belongs to me.'"
Job 41:10b-11

At this point in the text Job gets it. He lays down his pride:

> "Then Job replied to the Lord: 'I know that
> you can do all things; no plan of yours can be
> thwarted. You asked, "Who is this that obscures
> my counsel without knowledge?" Surely I spoke
> of things I did not understand, things too
> wonderful for me to know. You said, "Listen
> now, and I will speak; I will question you, and
> you shall answer me." My ears had heard of
> you but now my eyes have seen you. Therefore
> I despise myself and repent in dust and ashes.'"
> Job 42:1-6

God was quick to forgive Job and bless him, but if you want to know how the story ends and what happened to Job from there, you will have to read the remainder of chapter forty-two for yourself. My point in sharing this story with you is that God owns everything. He has a purpose for everything. And He expects us to take responsibility for ourselves and for our selfish way of thinking. Nobody is perfect. We all make mistakes and sin against others. I cannot tell you how many times I have come to God and said, "I despise myself and repent in dust and ashes." I have had to apologize to my own children numerous times over the years. If we have done wrong, we need to make it right. And it starts with humility. I really like how Gary Thomas describes how humility is wanting others to know us as we are. The truth is that none of us is perfect: "Humility is at root a celebration of our freedom in Christ; we are freed from having to make a certain impression or create a false front. Humility places within us a desire for people to know us as we are, not as we hope to be and not as we think they want us to be or even as we think we should be.

Real growth cannot begin until we come to this point." (139) In Romans chapter twelve, the Apostle Paul writes, "Live in harmony with one another. Do not be proud, but be willing to associate with people of low position. Do not be conceited. Do not repay anyone evil for evil. Be careful to do what is right in the eyes of everybody. If it is possible, as far as it depends on you, live at peace with everyone." (12:16-18)

You might ask, "But what if I ask for forgiveness and the other person refuses to forgive me?" That is not your problem. When you lay down your pride and tell them that you are sorry, you have just passed the ball to them. You have done your part. Remember "as far as it depends on you…" You cannot make peace with everyone. Some people won't let that happen. Maybe they just thrive on drama. Maybe they are so full of pride themselves they won't forgive. You can rest assured that you have done all you can to keep the peace.

FOURTEEN

The Power of Prayer

We look upon prayer as a means of getting
things for ourselves; the Bible's
idea of prayer is that we may get to know God Himself.
—*My Utmost for His Highest* by Oswald Chambers

When in my early twenties, I read two books that blew my eyes wide open in regard to prayer. *This Present Darkness* and *Piercing the Darkness* by Frank Peretti made a huge impact on me. Although they are fiction, these books taught me that spiritual warfare is real. That prayer makes a difference. Remember in my dream how my caregiver tried telling young mama that it was not the medicine allowing me to do those miraculous things? She said that because it was really prayers that gave me the power to be who God created me to be. I know for certain there are at least six godly women who have prayed for me throughout my life. And many of them still do. These ladies include two grandmas, one aunt, my daycare provider, my spiritual mom, Jennifer, and my second mom, Mercy. I believe the prayers of these women have allowed me to become the woman I am today. I am afraid to even think what may have become of me if it weren't for these amazing women and their faith.

I'm so glad that I learned the value of prayer at a young age. I have devoted much of my life to prayer, Biblical reading, and meditation. I know that if a person wants to have hope and be free, he must commit himself to these three things. There is no substitute for daily time spent in prayer, reading the Bible, and meditating on what you have read. Just like with any relationship, spending time with God really is the only way to develop a deep relationship with Him.

There is so much to learn about prayer, and I'm only able to touch on a few points here in this chapter. Throughout the new testament, Paul exhorts us to be devoted to prayer and to pray continually:

* Ephesians 6:18 "And pray in the Spirit on all occasions with all kinds of prayers and requests."
* I Thessalonians 5:16-17 "Be joyful always; pray continually; give thanks in all circumstances."
* Philippians 4:6 "Do not be anxious about anything, but in everything, by prayer and petition, with thanksgiving, present your requests to God."
* Colossians 4:2 "Devote yourselves to prayer, being watchful and thankful."

I find that as long as I keep God the main thing in my life, talking to Him comes easily. Whether I am in the car, on the job, or sitting quietly in my living room, I talk to Him. Sometimes I just thank Him for all He has done for me. Sometimes I ask for little things like a good parking spot when I am not feeling well. Sometimes I talk to Him about major life decisions like finding a job or asking forgiveness for my sin. We don't ever have to be hesitant to bring our requests to God. He is our creator and knows us inside and out.

There is so much to learn from the Bible for those of us who believe. In 2 Timothy 3:16, Paul explains to Timothy that "All scripture is God-breathed and is useful for teaching, rebuking, correcting and training in righteousness." And throughout the Bible, from cover to cover, we see examples of people praying and the prayers they said. I love to find these prayers of others and make them my own. For example, when I am in need of knowledge and wisdom, I turn to the following three passages and make them my own:

* Philippians 1:6-11 "that he who began a good work in (me) will carry it on to completion until the day of Christ Jesus...And this is my prayer: that (my) love may abound more and more in knowledge and depth of insight, so that (I) may be able to discern what is best and may be pure and blameless until the day of Christ, filled with the fruit of righteousness that comes through Jesus Christ—to the glory and praise of God."

* Colossians 1: 9-14 "asking God to fill (me) with the knowledge of his will through all spiritual wisdom and understanding. And (I) pray this in order that (I) may live a life worthy of the Lord and may please him in every way: bearing fruit in every good work, growing in the knowledge of God, being strengthened with all power according to his glorious might so that (I) may have great endurance and patience, and joyfully giving

thanks to the Father, who has qualified (me) to share in the inheritance of the saints in the kingdom of light. For he has rescued (me) from the dominion of darkness and brought (me) into the kingdom of the Son he loves, in whom (I) have redemption, the forgiveness of sins."

* Ephesians 1:17-19 "I keep asking that the God of our Lord Jesus Christ, the glorious Father, may give (me) the Spirit of wisdom and revelation, so that (I) may know him better. I pray also that the eyes of (my) heart may be enlightened in order that (I) may know the hope to which he has called (me), the riches of his glorious inheritance in the saints, and his incomparably great power for us who believe."

Proverbs 2 assures us that if we diligently seek wisdom, we will find it. I don't know about you, but I want to gain knowledge and wisdom all the days of my life. I don't like the idea of the alternative. Proverbs 10 compares wisdom to foolishness: "The wise in heart accept commands, but a chattering fool comes to ruin...Wise men store up knowledge, but the mouth of a fool invites ruin...The lips of the righteous nourish many, but fools die for lack of judgment...A fool finds pleasure in evil conduct, but a man of understanding delights in wisdom." (10:8-23) We all have the choice to be wise or to be a fool.

James 5:16 states "The prayer of a righteous man is powerful and effective." I've seen it happen. For example, one of my friends wanted to have a baby and it just was not happening. After praying for her for several years, she finally brought home a healthy baby boy. Today that baby boy is 18 years old. It might takes years to come to fruition, but God hears our prayers and does answer. Sometimes His answer is "no" and sometimes it is "yes." But then there are times when He answers with "not yet." Our job is to keep the faith and believe He has the best in store for us and those for whom we pray.

The apostle Paul knew the power of prayer first hand. In his letter to the Ephesians he writes, "I kneel before the Father…I pray that out of his glorious riches he may strengthen you with power through his Spirit in your inner being…I pray that you, being rooted and established in love, may have power… to grasp how wide and long and high and deep is the love of Christ, and to know this love that surpasses knowledge—that you may be filled to the measure of all the fullness of God." (3:14-19) He was praying for their relationships with God. He wanted them to grow spiritually and continue to seek the Lord. This is what our Lord wants from us as well.

In the Old Testament the prophet Jeremiah shares these words: "'For I know the plans I have for you,' declares the Lord, 'plans to prosper you and not to harm you, plans to give you hope and a future. Then you will call upon me and come and pray to me, and I will listen to you. You will seek me and find me when you seek me with all your heart. I will be found by you,' declares the Lord, 'and will bring you back from captivity. I will gather you from all the nations and places where I have banished you,' declares the Lord, 'and will bring you back to the place from which I carried you into exile.'" (29:11-14) God wants us to go to Him whole-heartily and every day, not just now and again when we might really need something. He listens, and we can be sure that He takes note of every single prayer ever lifted to Him.

Sometimes I get very weary from asking God for healing. When I'm in excruciating pain, all I can do is silently scream, "Jesus. Jesus. Jesus." And what really helps me is knowing that God has sent His Holy Spirit to help. In Romans 8:26 Paul tells us, "The Spirit helps us in our weakness. We do not know what we ought to pray for, but the Spirit himself intercedes for us with groans that words cannot express." Take heart, my friend, in times of great need, and when you have run out of words to say, the Holy Spirit takes your requests to God.

One thing that helps me settle into my time with God in prayer is this little quote by Mama Maggie Cobran: "Silence your body to listen to your words. Silence your tongue to listen to your thoughts. Silence your thoughts to listen to your heart. Silence your heart to listen to your spirit. Silence your spirit to listen to His Spirit." What this does is help weed out the distractions. We need a quiet space to commune with and hear from God. Many years ago I heard a sermon that has helped me in my prayer times. We were told to "Ask for: Grace—for when I am weak, Mercy—for when I wander, Peace—for when I am weary."

Maybe you are wondering how you can avoid reading your Bible every day. Maybe you don't like to read or just have too many other things to do. I've heard all of the excuses, trust me. Sometimes I will take a Bible verse that is speaking to me, and I'll write it on a 3x5 card. I'll tape it to my dashboard or on my bathroom mirror. I'll read it over and over again until I have it memorized. Maybe you take fifteen minutes every morning to drink your coffee. You could spend those waking moments praying and reading. Maybe you would rather listen to the Bible. There are many great Bibles and spiritual books on audio. Check it out. But don't make any more excuses. You will never be sorry for the time you spend in prayer, reading the Bible, and meditating.

Maybe you are wondering how anyone can hear from God. It is in the quiet moments that He speaks to me. I hear a small quiet voice in the back of my head that gives me direction. He also speaks to me through His Word—The Bible, as well as through spiritual writings of other Christians. I have included a reading list in the back of this book to help you as you seek to know God better. Knowing God's Word is indispensable to our spiritual growth. Joni Eareckson Tada asks her readers, "Have we really grasped this link between getting our prayers answered and steeping our minds in Christ's words? The longer the tea bag sits in the cup, the stronger the tea. The more God's word saturates our minds, the clearer our grasp on what's important to him and the stronger our prayers." (63, *When God Weeps*) There really is no other way you can do it. One of my pastors always says, "Hug your Bible every day." When we fall in love with God, we also fall in love with His Word. Gary Thomas explains how learning to love God will lead us into great things: "when we learn to love the Lord our God with all our hearts, soul, mind, and strength (Mark 12:30) then holiness will be the by-product of our passion. We cease from sin, not just because we are disciplined, but because we have found something better." (68)

As for meditation, I cannot explain it any better than to quote J.I. Packer. In his book, *Knowing God* he writes, "Meditation is the activity of calling to mind, and thinking over, and dwelling on, and applying to oneself, the various things that one knows about the words and ways and purposes and promises of God. It is an activity of holy thought, consciously performed in the presence of God, under the eye of God, by the help of God, as a means of communion with God. Its purpose is to clear one's mental and spiritual vision of God, and to let his truth make its full and proper impact on one's mind and heart. It is a matter of talking to oneself about God and oneself; it is, indeed, often a matter of arguing with oneself, reasoning oneself out of moods of doubt and unbelief into a clear apprehension of God's power and grace. Its effect is ever to humble us, as we contemplate God's greatness and glory and our own littleness and sinfulness, and to encourage and reassure us—'comfort' us, in the old, strong, Bible sense of the word—as we contemplate the unsearchable riches of divine mercy displayed in the Lord Jesus Christ." (23)

So reading, praying, and meditating—sounds easy, right? Wrong! There is nothing easy about it. I read one time that in order to develop a good habit we have to do it for twenty-one consecutive days. Then it will become easier and easier. Give it a try. And if you fail, try again. Just never stop trying.

There is one last thing about reading/listening to the Word of God (the Bible). James, the brother of Jesus, tells us, "Do not merely listen to the word, and so deceive yourselves. Do what is says. Anyone who listens to the word but does not do what it says is like a man who looks at his face in a mirror and, after looking at himself, goes away and immediately forgets what he looks like. But the man who looks intently into the perfect law that gives freedom, and continues to do this, not forgetting what he has heard, but doing it—he will be blessed in what he does." (James 1:22-25) Read it. Pray and meditate on it. Do it. Period. And you will be blessed; I promise.

FIFTEEN

Hope

We who have fled to take hold of the hope
offered to us may be greatly encouraged.
We have this hope as an anchor for the soul, firm and secure.
—Hebrews 6:18-19

At times my life is "normal": the sun will shine, the birds will sing, and everything is wonderful. But then, without warning, The Storm comes. And my world comes to a halt. Worse than that actually. As I grew older I began to get bitter about how much of my life has been lost to The Storm, for I am laid up for days at a time—just enduring. Just enduring the incessant pain. And it is taking a toll on my body.

The Bible tells us to rejoice in our sufferings. The Bible says to *"rejoice in our sufferings?"* This sounds ludicrous! The first time I heard it I thought the pastor must have quoted a verse incorrectly. As I read it for myself, I saw that it really does say this. Although I read it for myself in black and white, and although I believed the Bible to be God's perfect word, I did not understand.

As I grew up I searched God's heart about suffering, and He began to reveal the awesome power behind the words written by His servant Paul. I read that Paul wrote to the Roman people in 57 AD, but I realized these words were also written to me and everyone who hears the word. I began to understand how the command to "rejoice in sufferings" is followed by an explanation as to why we should rejoice. The rest of the passage tells how "suffering produces perseverance; perseverance, character; and character, hope." (Romans 5:3-5) I started thinking about these other things and realized how I had become rich in these areas of my life, all as a result of suffering.

It has taken many years to learn the value of suffering, and sometimes I am unable to rejoice in the pain. For fifty years I have struggled, and for fifty years I have not lost hope. God has poured out His love on me that I might not lose hope. Through all of the pain and suffering, I have persevered and been able to hold onto hope.

In my late twenties I was being attacked by storm after storm and trying to rejoice. I was struggling to hold onto hope, and this is what I wrote:

"What Else?"

Never give up!—Yes, this is what I believe; this is what has kept me going year after year. But I sure feel like giving up right now. I hate this feeling. It hits me every time. Three more days of my life gone. I wonder how many months or maybe even years have just disappeared from

119

my life. Months that have been wasted while I lay in bed, as I sleep away the days—waiting for the pain to let up.

Dear God, will this nightmare ever end? I don't think I can live the rest of my life this way. I have so many desires, dreams, responsibilities—I know, when I am weak, you are strong. I just wonder how much pain and sickness my body can withstand. Although I am only twenty-nine, the pain and sickness has taken its toll. How much more can I take?—Yes, I also know that you will never allow me to bear more than I can handle.

My heart is so heavy, my mind so cloudy, my head so tight, and my limbs so weak. God, I beg you—take it away! Do I need more faith? Do I need to keep searching for an answer? I do trust you, Lord. Year after year I have struggled—I dare not think where else I might go—but to you. You are my only hope!

Joni Eareckson Tada has been one of my heroes since I was a teenager and saw her movie. Her book, *When God Weeps*, has been such an encouragement to me. In the introduction, her co-author establishes that the book "is about God weeping over human heartache, his entering our anguish himself, and the *love* that drives him to let us suffer. It's about experiencing the friendship of God along difficult paths we didn't even know he walked." Joni continues the introduction by hoping the reader "will better understand why our weeping matters to a loving God. A God who, one day, will make clear the meaning behind every tear. Even his tears."

If anyone has had to fight to keep the faith, it is Joni. If you don't know her story, I encourage you to learn more about her. She admits that "Faith is hard." And that "We can't see the good flowing from our heartaches." (92) She continues by explaining, "Believers who face the greatest conflict yet hold on to God with all their hearts, at times clinging to hope like the string of a kite." (106) She has been and continues to be in the trenches of suffering. Joni most certainly knows how hard it is to hold on.

The writer of Hebrews also knew about suffering. He encourages us to "hold unswervingly to the hope we profess, for he who promised is faithful." He goes on to say, "But we are not of those who shrink back and are destroyed, but of those who believe and are saved." (Hebrews 10: 23,39) He encourages us to keep fighting, and we will be saved out of our suffering.

In his letter to the Galatians, the apostle Paul also encourages us to keep the faith: "Let us not become weary in doing good, for at the proper time we will reap a harvest if we do not give up." (Galatians 6:9) The Bible doesn't answer all of our why questions, but we can be assured that our suffering does not go unnoticed by our Lord. Jesus himself teaches us that we are blessed: "Blessed are you who weep now, for you will laugh." (Luke 6:21) There is hope in His words, my friends. I like the way Joni explains God's "arithmetic." She says, "Jesus seemed to make it a 'minus' rather than a 'plus'—gaining-through-losing arithmetic." (180)

She goes on to explain how the apostle Paul applied this same arithmetic to his life: "Paul's arithmetic for contentment was to subtract his earthly wants so that something of greater value could be attained: Christ's cause advanced throughout the world. This gave him enormous joy. Joy based on his conviction that suffering Christians are used more powerfully in God's kingdom. And when he was thrown into prison the next time—and for the last time—he was rejoicing greatly." (178) And in his second letter to the Corinthians, Paul encourages them to be "sorrowful, yet always rejoicing; poor, yet making many rich; having nothing, and yet possessing everything." Gary Thomas encourages us: "The barrenness of these spiritual deserts can be excruciating. When we face them it will be an encouragement for us to realize that others, in fact most Christians, have experienced, to one degree or another, what we are experiencing. We are not abnormal or less committed Christians for going through this dry spell. We do not need to uncover buried sins that are stealing our joy. We are simply average Christians going through a normal spiritual process." (191, *Seeking the Face of God*)

So how can we apply this type of arithmetic to our own lives? First we need to realize that through our suffering God is drawing us to Himself. It's about our relationship with Him. He wants us to give ourselves to Him. Just like the poem "Footprints in the Sand," it is at the hardest times in life when God wants to pick us up and carry us through. But it is our choice to let Him carry us or not. It is in our despair (or *Black Night of the Soul* if you will) when a "vertical line to God opens us up to change, real hope, and the possibility of seeing God as he really is, not as we want him to be." (157, *When God Weeps*)

One of the most important things I have taken away from Joni's testimony is a practical application of how to hold on when deep in the despair. She tells us, "Never doubt in the darkness what you once believed in the light. When hardship settles in to stay, dark and brooding skepticism surges over us in a tide of doubt and fear. The only sure dike against a flood of feelings is *memory*. We must recall sunnier times when we drove deep the pilings of God's goodness and felt our moorings of trust hold ground. Times when we lived on his blessings, knew his favor, were grateful for his gifts, and felt the flesh and blood of his everlasting arms underneath us." (161) If you are currently experiencing the sunnier times, don't hesitate. Now is the time to develop a deep relationship with the Lord. You never know when your *Dark Night* will come. You could lose your spouse or child in a car accident tomorrow. Maybe your next doctor's appointment reveals cancer in your body. Or you come home from work next week to find your spouse has left you for someone else. Will we draw closer to God in our time of need, or push Him away? Again, it's our choice.

One of my favorite passages is in Romans where Paul goes into detail about what hope is, and how we can have hope: "For in this hope we were saved. But hope that is seen is no hope at all. Who hopes for what he already has? But if we hope for what we do not yet have, we wait for it patiently." (Romans 8:24-25)

No matter how much pain or suffering we go through, no matter how hard life is, we must not lose hope. Hope is God and our only hope is God. Because of this fact, we must seek Him with all of our hearts and accept His love, then we will be able to rejoice in our sufferings. Today I thank the Lord for loving me so much that he has helped me persevere, develop character, keep hope alive in my spirit, and be able to rejoice in my sufferings.

SIXTEEN

Freedom

Freedom in Christ is not freedom to
sin, but freedom from sin—
freedom to live as God intends, in truth and holiness.
—*Slave: The Hidden Truth About Your Identity
in Christ* by John MacArthur

In the second part of the dream I had, there was the young mama asleep in a bed and the old mama asleep in the other bed. The young mama was asleep because my mom is no longer young and I am grown. My mom as a young woman does not have a voice in my life anymore, and that is why she is asleep in the dream. Although she doesn't have an audible voice in my life, I still hear her voice sometimes. For instance, whenever I do something clumsy, like spill something, I still hear her voice in the back of my head telling me that I am such a klutz. She used to tell me that all the time when I was growing up. My mom was an old woman when she died; she was eighty-four. The old mama in my dream was asleep because she no longer has a voice in my life either. It has been more than nine years since I wrote the note and left it on her kitchen table.

That night when I wrote the note, I also made the decision to free myself from my mom's control. I was determined to keep her from hurting me again. It took quite awhile, but now I only hear her voice in the back of my head on occasion. I've been really working at shutting down those voices when they start to torment me. Like my therapist suggested, I speak back to those negative messages and tell them that they speak lies, and I do not believe them. I'm learning to resist their power to steal my joy. Some of those negative messages are: you are not good enough, you can't do that, you're too clumsy. The truth that I shoot back at them is that I AM good enough, I CAN do that, and it's OK to be clumsy. All of these things are true because the Bible says so. As I have grown closer to Christ, I've learned that my self-confidence and self-worth are based on Christ alone. It is His power in me that makes me good enough and allows me to do whatever I want to do.

John 10:10 says, "The thief comes only to steal and kill and destroy; I have come that they may have life, and have it to the full." The thief is Satan. And it is Jesus who has come to give us a full life of joy. I believe that Satan uses other people to get to us sometimes. His negative messages came through my mom to steal my joy. But I am putting a stop to it and will not allow Him to do this anymore. I don't know who wrote the following quote, but I love it and use it to speak to the thief: "The Devil whispered in my ear, 'You're not strong enough to withstand the storm.' I answered back, 'I am a child of God, a woman of faith, a warrior of Christ. I am the storm!'" It's so important to stop believing and listening to the lies that the enemy wants us to believe. If you want to know the truth, go to God's Word. John 14:27 tells us, "Peace I leave with you; my peace I give you. I do not give to you as the world gives. Do not let your hearts be troubled and do not be afraid." If your heart is troubled by a person in your life, you need to really evaluate whether they are building you up or tearing you down. Maybe it's time to find a new friend. Or maybe you need to talk to them about it.

Another person I had to walk away from was my second husband. Roger was always yelling at me and telling me I was stupid, ugly, etc. The enemy used Roger to steal all of my joy at that time. I became a little mouse of woman. He had me isolated in a place with no car and no money. He had no respect for me and didn't seem to care about me at all. Roger was a big man with large muscles from lifting weights. Not only was I beaten down by him verbally, but I was also afraid of him. He never did lay a hand on me, but he certainly abused me in every other possible way. He would get angry and punch things. One time he punched his fist clear through our coffee table.

Just like I am learning to do with my mom's negative messages, after the divorce, it took me a long time to get Roger's voice out of my head. It actually took me about two years to recover from his abuse and become myself again. I will be sharing more about domestic abuse in the next chapter.

I am so pleased to be free from the torment of my mom and from Roger. Another freedom that we have in Christ is freedom from fear. When the divorce from Roger was final, I was free from the fear I had of him. The Bible has a lot to say about fear and how we can be free from it. We must believe that God is bigger than any fear we might have. I struggle with this in regard to my fear of snakes. I don't think that one will ever go away. The prophet Isaiah had a lot to say about fear:

"I have chosen you and have not rejected you; So do not fear, for I am with you; do not be dismayed, for I am your God. I will strengthen you and help you; I will uphold you with my righteous right hand...For I am the Lord, your God, who takes hold of your right hand and says to you, Do not fear; I will help you." (41:9-13) In the New Testament you will find that Jesus taught his disciples a lot about peace. One of those verses is John 16:33: "I have told you these things, so that in me you may have peace. In this world you will have trouble. But take heart! I have overcome the world." He doesn't say we will be free of trouble, but He does assure us that in Him we will find peace. And this is exactly Thomas' point when he writes, "Again, a holy passion for God is the primary antidote. Consistently, we are told to run, as a little child would run, into the Father's arms. Fenelon taught that we should act like a small child who, when shown something horrible, 'only recoils from it and buries himself in his mother's breast, so that he will see nothing. The practice of the presence of God is the supreme remedy. It sustains. It comforts. It calms.'" (69, *Seeking the Face of God*)

And finally, in Christ we can find freedom from sin. God wants us to live in truth and holiness. This is where true happiness comes from. If we will continue to seek God and be faithful to repent of our sins, He will forgive us. There truly is freedom in that. Paul explains it well in Romans 8:1, "Therefore, there is now no condemnation for those who are in Christ Jesus, because through Christ Jesus the law of the Spirit of life set me free from the law of sin and death." The law of sin and death is the result of what took place in the Garden of Eden. Because man sinned, he needed to be punished. But thankfully, Jesus came to change all of that. He came to earth to take our sin upon Himself. He took our punishment. And for those of us who believe, we are set free from eternal punishment and death. That is the hope we have in Christ and in Christ alone.

Is it easy to be free from sin? Absolutely not. There are battles that every Christian goes through. We still get tempted and have to battle our sinful desires. Paul wrote to the people of Galatia about this battle: "So I say, live by the Spirit, and you will not gratify the desires of the sinful nature. For the sinful nature desires what is contrary to the Spirit, and the Spirit what is contrary to the sinful nature. They are in conflict with each other, so that you do not do what you want." (Galatians 5:16-18) When we are tempted, we need to resist and ask God for help. His power in us is strong enough to overcome any temptation. I hope you will embrace Christ and choose freedom.

SEVENTEEN

Domestic Abuse

Some of the strongest women I know are
those who have escaped an abusive
marriage, clinging to God's hand every step of the way.
—Author Unknown

What do you think of when you hear the term domestic abuse? Do you think of violence within a marriage or intimate relationship? As stated by The Fight Against Domestic Violence organization (fadv.org), domestic violence is the "willful intimidation, physical assault, battery, sexual assault, and/or other abusive behavior as part of a systematic pattern of power and control perpetrated by one intimate partner against another. It includes physical violence, sexual violence, psychological violence, and emotional abuse. The frequency and severity of domestic violence can vary dramatically;

however, the one constant component of domestic violence is one partner's consistent efforts to maintain power and control over the other. Domestic violence is underfunded and under-discussed in society. The violence is normalized and even seen as inevitable in many popular films, songs, and other media. According to the National Coalition Against Domestic Violence (NCADV), one in three women and one in four men will be victims of intimate partner violence in their lifetimes in the United States alone."

FADV goes on to give resources for those in need of help: "If you are in immediate danger, please call 911. If you live in the United States, and you need anonymous, confidential help, 24/7, please call the National Domestic Violence Hotline at 1-800-799-7233 (SAFE) or 1-800-787-3224 (TTY). You are the best judge of your situation and you know your partner best. If you are in an unsafe situation, and you are being abused, please remember that you are not to blame, you have nothing to be ashamed of, and that there is hope and help. If you decide to take action, there are many tools and resources to support you. You can find a list of domestic violence service providers and learn more about the topic of domestic violence at the National Network to End Domestic Violence and at Domestic Shelters. You can also use online tools to assess the danger level of your situation and to develop a safety plan to help you prepare to leave the relationship, if you choose to do so."

Physical violence is only a part of domestic abuse. Abuse can come in many forms. And it crosses over from intimate partners to other relationships including parent/child, uncle or aunt/child, between siblings, between close friends, etc. And domestic abuse can include any of the following:

* Emotional abuse and intimidation (yelling and shouting at the victim, blaming the victim for their own abuse, threatening with weapons, abuses or threatens to abuse pets, controlling who the victim sees and talks to, humiliation publicly or privately, throwing and breaking things in the house.)
* Sexual abuse (forcing the victim to have sex, demanding particular sex acts, waking the victim in the middle of the night for sex, bullying the victim with accusations of cheating.)
* Economic abuse (limiting the victim's access to money, preventing victim from getting or keeping a job, keeping the victim on an allowance, makes the victim ask for money, controlling the victim's access to family finances.)
* Coercion and threats (forcing the victim to drop abuse charges, threatening to commit suicide, threatening to abandon the family, threatening to harm or take away the children, threatening to carry out physical harm, using guilt and mind games to control the victim.)

Whether it is physical, mental, emotional, verbal, sexual, or economic abuse, if we could see into every person's spirit to see the wounds and hurts, we would be in shock as to how many of us have those wounds and scars. I don't claim to have all of the answers, but my heart hurts and wants to help those in need and to help them heal. I would like to see the church step up to the plate and equip its members in how to help those in abusive situations and/or to help them heal from the abuse. It is time to get the conversation started. People should be comfortable and safe to go to the church for help. And it is paramount the church does screening and does not bring into leadership those who have been abusive. I know of too many people who have been abused by church leaders, Sunday school teachers, and the church community. That needs to stop!

If you know someone who is being abused, you must trust their ability to make their own choices. They know the abuser best, and they are the best judge of their situation. But you can be a supportive friend and ally by being a listening ear and by knowing the resources available in your area. Here are a few tips:

* Be an active listener without judgment.
* Validate and comfort them with comments like, "I'm so sorry that happened to you." and "This was not your fault." and "I'm here for you."
* Ask what you can do to help. Instead of pushing someone to action, ask how you can support them in their choices.
* Know your local and national resources. Educate yourself so you can offer options and leave space for someone to make their own decisions.

One of my favorite books is called *Boundaries* by Dr Henry Cloud and Dr John Townsend. This book has really helped me understand and set boundaries in my life. These authors begin their book by explaining why boundaries are important: "Boundaries help us to distinguish our property so that we can take care of it. They help us to 'guard our heart with all diligence.' We need to keep things that will nurture us inside our fences and keep things that will harm us outside. In short, *boundaries help us keep the good in and the bad out*. They guard our treasures (Matt. 7:6) so that people will not steal them. They keep the pearls inside, and the pigs outside." (33)

The authors stress the importance of having a good support system in place when you start setting boundaries with the abusive person. Because our most basic need is for relationships, victims often suffer through the abuse because they are afraid they will be left all alone. But a good support system can offer them strength, love, and support as they start to set limits.

Setting boundaries is not easy. Cloud and Townsend warn that it can cause the abuser to attack or withdraw. We have no control over how the abuser will respond. The important thing is to have a plan in place in case this happens. On the flip side, the abuser may welcome the boundaries and see them as a way to better the relationship.

You need to know that there is freedom is setting boundaries. The authors describe this on page 118: "Finally, as you develop a sense of biblical boundaries, you develop more safety in the present. You develop more confidence. You are less enslaved to the fear of other people." And on page 163: "People who set limits exhibit self-control and show responsibility for themselves. They act responsible to their partner by confronting him or her. Setting limits is an act of love in the marriage; by binding and limiting the evil, they protect the good."

But what if the abuser becomes angry? "The angry person has a character problem. If you reinforce this character problem, it will return tomorrow and the next day in other situations. It is not the situation that's making the person angry, but the feeling that they are entitled to things from others. They want to control others and, as a result, they have no control over themselves. So, when they lose their wished-for control over someone, they 'lose it.' They get angry. The first thing you need to learn is that the person who is angry at you for setting boundaries is the one with the problem." (247-248, *Boundaries*)

The authors go on to explain that "Boundaries without consequences are not boundaries. You must decide if you are willing to enforce the consequences before you set the boundaries." (254) In regard to resistance, some people are afraid to set boundaries because they may become physically overpowered. "They are often afraid that they will get beaten worse if they tell. They must realize the seriousness of the problem and get outside help. The problem will not go away, and it could get a lot worse. If you are in this situation, find other people to help you set limits on the abuse. Find a counselor who has dealt with abusive spouses before. Arrange to call people in your church if your spouse or friend gets violent. Arrange for a place to stay overnight if you are threatened, no matter the hour. Call the police and an attorney. Get a restraining order on such an individual if he will respect no other limit. Do it for yourself and for your children. Do not allow this to go on. Seek help." (255)

Finally, I want to address marriage specifically. Since I was abused by Roger, and I have befriended numerous women in abusive marriages, my heart aches for those women specifically. Many husbands like to throw the submission verse at their wives. What they leave out is that they too are to be submissive to their wives. Ephesians 5:21 says, "Submit to one another out of reverence for Christ." And after this verse, Paul goes on to explain how not only are wives to submit to their husbands, but the husband is to love the wife "just as Christ loved the church and gave himself up for her to make her holy." (v. 25) Christ gave his very life out of love for the church and so that we could be holy. An abusive husband is doing anything but loving his wife.

When I was meeting with my friend Echo, she would often remind me of the following verse: "If anyone does not provide for his relatives, and especially for his immediate family, he has denied the faith and is worse than an unbeliever." (I Timothy 5:8) She told me that only if Roger started working and providing for the needs of my family, should I even consider going back to him. He was not working, and he would not allow me to work. JD Gunter is a staff member at The Southern Baptist Theological Seminary and he says, "Whatever a man thinks he is 'called' to, this much is clear—he is called to provide for his family. One of the most God-glorifying pictures of the gospel is when a man puts his childhood dreams to the side, steps up to the plate, gets a job, and valiantly cares for his family. This man should be honored and his work should be appreciated."

Once I was out of that marriage, and again when I was out of my relationship with my mom, I realized that I needed to replace those negative voices with the voice of truth. One of my favorite worship songs is called *The Voice of Truth* by Casting Crowns. I have come back to these lyrics time and time again as I work on listening to God's voice instead of man's: "And they laugh at me, reminding me of all the times I've tried before and failed. You'll never win. But the Voice of Truth tells me a different story. The Voice of Truth says do not be afraid. Out of all the voices calling out to me, I will choose to listen and believe the Voice of Truth."

In order to prevent being abused by anyone, I think it is important to remember this: "Never tolerate disrespect. The more chances you give someone the less respect they'll start to have for you. They'll begin to ignore the standards that you've set because they'll know another chance will always be given. They're not afraid to lose you because they know no matter what you won't walk away. They get comfortable with depending on your forgiveness. Never let a person get comfortable disrespecting you." (https://dailyinspirationalquotes.in)

EIGHTEEN

Mental Illness

All it takes is a beautiful fake smile to
hide an injured soul and they
will never notice how broken you really are.
—Robin Williams

As you can imagine, domestic abuse often leaves the victim
to deal with depression and anxiety. For the three years I was
married to Roger I was depressed most of the time. And I was
always anxious about where our next meal would come from,
when he would blow up again, and how we would pay the
next month's rent. Having chronic pain often leads to mental
illnesses as well. While dealing with the chronic migraines all
of my life, depression has come right along with them. And the
anxiety of always wondering when the next attack will occur
is also a problem. I rarely leave my home without wondering if

I will have to get back right away in case the over-the-counter meds on hand do not help. Along with abuse and pain, there are other circumstances that will lead a person to develop a mental illness. Several times throughout my life I've dealt with loneliness and discouragement, and that did not help my depression. Finally, I also have genetics going against me. Several of my family members also suffer with mental illness. In fact when I was a teenager, one of my uncles died by suicide.

I do not claim to be a doctor and want to encourage you, if you are suffering from a mental illness, please seek professional help. There is no shame in going to a psychologist for help dealing with these crippling illnesses. And if you are thinking suicidal thoughts, please call 911 and ask for help. Another great resource is the National Suicide Prevention Lifeline: 800-273-8255

According to the National Alliance of Mental Illness (nami. org) five of the most common mental illnesses include: anxiety, depression, bipolar, eating disorders, and substance abuse. As of 2015, about one in five adults experienced a mental illness in a given year. Suicide is the tenth leading cause of death in the United States, with eighteen to twenty-two military veterans taking their own lives every day.

The statistics are overwhelming. And my heart aches for everyone suffering with these lonely, often hidden illnesses. So many times we are shocked when we hear of someone who has taken his or her own life. It is always a shock. We wonder how a person could get that bad. But if you have been there yourself, you understand. I'm glad that the conversation has started, but there needs to be more. The church needs to equip its members to handle these situations. People should not be afraid to talk about their struggles. The church should be a safe place. People like me just need friends and family to love them unconditionally.

Writing this chapter is the most difficult for me. Even now I am struggling with the flood waters of depression. Not only am I writing this for you, the reader, but also for myself. You and I need to go to a family member, friend, or therapist to help us deal with our mental illness. If we can just go to one person and say, "I need help," I believe we can start to manage our illness better.

God knows us intimately and he understands when we struggle. The Bible actually has much to say about anxiety:

* "An anxious heart weighs a man down, but a kind word cheers him up." Proverbs 12:25 (How about if we all start saying kind words to one another? We never know what the other person might be struggling with.)
* "Do not be anxious about anything, but in everything, by prayer and petition, with thanksgiving, present your requests to God." Philippians 4:6 (It is not always easy, but with practice, and with Christ's help, we can begin to leave our worries with God and trust that He will work everything out.)
* "Cast all your anxiety on him because he cares for you." I Peter 5:7
* "Therefore I tell you, do not worry about your life, what you will eat or drink; or about your body, what you will wear. Is not life more important than food, and the body more important than clothes? Look at the birds of the air; they do not sow or reap or store away in barns, and yet your heavenly Father feeds them. Are you not much more valuable than they? Who of you by worrying can add a single hour to his life?" Matthew 6:25-27

These scripture passages are an assurance that God understands our struggle. And we can always go to Him for peace and comfort. Joni Eareckson Tada talks about worry as Jesus confronted it in one of his sermons:

> "Sometimes I look up on my wall calendar and gaze at the blank months of years to come and I wonder, *'What will it be like five years from now? Ten years? What if my husband suffers an injury and can't take care of me? Worse yet, I won't be able to take care of him!'* The enemy of contentment is worry. In Jesus's Sermon on the Mount, the phrase he repeated most often was, 'Do not worry.' The Lord was wise in repeating his warnings so many times. He knows the devastating affects of anxiety and how it can corrode faith like acid; robbing you of joy and stealing your hope. I'm sure this is why Jesus said in the same sermon, 'Therefore do not worry about tomorrow, for tomorrow will worry about itself. *Each day has enough trouble of its own'* (Matthew 6:34). The secret of being content is to take one day at a time. Not five years or ten at a time, but one day." (184, *When God Weeps*)

I read an article recently called *Me and the Black Dog* by Theresa E. Miedema. She makes a very good point that it is ok to ask someone if they are ok. It has really resonated with me as I can relate so much to what she says about depression:

"Physiologically, depression hurts. It physically hurts...It feels like my soul is dying. Maybe it is: depression is a cancer of the soul...

You feel angry. You feel irritable. You feel despondent. And then you don't feel at all...

One of the ways you can help people with depression is by being present. Just be there and don't offer advice...

If you are not sure if someone is okay, ask... You can ask, 'Are you okay?' Or, 'Would you like to have coffee together? Or would you care to join me on a walk?' Be a tool of hope; don't tritely suggest that 'maybe more prayer would help.'"

In his book *Depression: A Stubborn Darkness*, Edward T. Welch exhorts us when he says, "Contrary to what we might think, God says that strong faith can coexist with emotional highs, lows, and everything in between. It is a myth that faith is always smiling. The truth is that faith often feels like the very ordinary process of dragging one foot in front of the other because we are conscious of God." (31) If you have been told that you can't be a Christian and have a mental illness, that is not true. Many of the great Bible characters struggled right along with us. Just like with any other illness, it is God's desire to heal us. But in the meantime, He wants us to come to Him and grow our relationship with Him:

"'Consider it pure joy, my brothers, whenever you face trials of many kinds, because you know that the testing of your faith develops perseverance. Perseverance must finish its work so that you may be mature and complete, not lacking anything.' (James 1:2-4) These are not the easiest of God's words to hear, and it would take some explanation to link them to your situation. But the absence of the word 'depression' (or insert your own mental illness here) shouldn't keep you from finding encouragement and purpose in this passage. James intentionally enlarges the scope of suffering—'trials of many kinds.' By doing this, he invites those who experience depression to learn that, whatever the cause, depression will reveal our faith and serve as a catalyst for growth rather than a reason for despair." (38)

Once again we can allow our trials (mental illness) to make us bitter or better. God wants you to be better. And by hanging onto our hope in Him, we will be better.

I like how Welch goes on to explain that not only can we become better, but we can also use our mental illness to help others: "A wise older counselor, who had experienced depression himself, challenged other depressed people this way: 'Fight the spiritual battles that accompany depression so that you can love other people.' It sounds simple, but it is the summary of many years of experience." (85) I feel as if I could have written those words myself. I've been on the battlefield with depression for fifty years, but can now say that I want to help others and love them through it. Use your mental illness to grow stronger in your faith, then reach out and help others who are also struggling.

CONCLUSION

I consider that our present sufferings
are not worth comparing with
the glory that will be revealed in us.
—Romans 8:18

Remember a few years back when mission statements were all the rage? Whether we were at work, school, or church, our leaders had us thinking about our missions and goals. I even created one with my kids for our family of three. We came up with a statement and added four points to help us accomplish our mission. I also added the Golden Rule at the bottom of the paper: "Do to others what you would have them do to you." Matthew 7:12. We all signed it; I laminated it and posted it on the cork board in our kitchen. I returned to this statement many times over my kids' growing up years.

Whether you have a personal statement, a Bible verse, or whatever, I think it is important to state your goals. If we don't have goals, who knows where we will end up. Maybe your goal is to get a "B" on your next exam. Maybe your goal is to become the CEO of your company. Maybe your goal is to buy a house in the next year. Personally, I have written and rewritten my goals over and over again throughout the years. This is because

"People can make all kinds of plans, but only the Lord's plan will happen." Proverbs 19:21. Like I mentioned earlier, listening to and learning from others has always been one of my goals. There is a cliche I really like because so many people are quick to give advice. It states: "An ounce of example is worth more than a ton of advice." Too many times I've heard people say one thing, but then do something else. I also like this cliche because it reminds me that my life is setting an example for those around me. And my goal is to have my example and my advice line up with each other. Another thing a mission statement will do is help you decide what is most important in your life.

It is my prayer that after reading this book you will choose to live a life of freedom and that you will live with hope. I also pray that you will choose the goal of heaven at the end of your life here on earth. This can easily be achieved by a few simple steps. In order to achieve our goals, we must make a game plan. The game plan to get to heaven includes believing, confessing, asking, accepting, and professing. First, we have to believe that God sent His only son, Jesus, to die on the cross for our sins. Second, we must profess our sins to God and ask for His forgiveness. Third, we must accept God's gift of unconditional love and sacrifice and ask Him to be Lord of our lives. And last, we must profess with our mouths that God is our Lord and Savior.

It is only through Jesus Christ that we are saved from the punishment we deserve. Jesus will come into your life and transform you into a new creation if you will just ask. Yes, it is that simple. I pray that you will choose salvation today and find freedom like you have never known before. Just like I did when I was eleven years old.

If you have any questions or just want to let me know how this book has impacted you, please feel free to email me at: Grace@GraceRockwell.com

SOURCES AND RECOMMENDED READING

Alcorn, Randy. *Heaven*. Tydale House Publishers Inc, 2004.

Chambers, Oswald. *My Utmost for His Highest*. Barbour Publishing, 1963.

Chapman, Gary. *The Five Love Languages: How to Express Heartfelt Commitment to Your Mate*. Northfield Publishing, 1995.

Cloud, Dr. Henry and Townsend, Dr. John. *Boundaries*. Zondervan, 1992.

Eareckson Tada, Joni and Estes, Steven. *When God Weeps*. Zondervan, 1997.

Eldredge, John. *Desire*. Thomas Nelson Inc, 2007.

Eldredge, John. *Walking with God*. Thomas Nelson Inc, 2008.

Eldredge, John. *Wild at Heart*. Thomas Nelson Inc, 2001.

Eldredge, John and Stasi. *Captivating*. Thomas Nelson Inc, 2005.

Golomb Ph.D., Elan. *Trapped in the Mirror: Adult Children of Narcissists in Their Struggle for Self*. Harper, 1992.

Hamon, Jane. *Dreams and Visions*. Regal Books, 2000.

Kempis, Thomas a. *The Imitation of Christ*. Doubleday, 1955.

Kline, Peggy. *Treating Yourself Like Royalty: Creating the Noble and Majestic Life you Deserve*. Winsome Press, 2008.

Miedema, Theresa E. *Me and the Black Dog.* https://www.thebanner.org/features/2019/04/me-and-the-black-dog

McGee, Robert S. *The Search for Significance.* Thomas Nelson Inc, 2003.

Moore, Beth. *A Woman and Her God.* Integrity Publishers, 2003.

Morgan, Elisa. *The Beauty of Broken: My Story, and likely Yours Too.* Thomas Nelson Inc, 2013.

Morgan, Elisa. *She Did What She Could Do: Five Words of Jesus That Will Change Your Life.* Tydale House Publishers Inc, 2009.

Packer, J.I. *Knowing God.* InterVarsity Press, 1973.

Peretti, Frank E. *Piercing the Darkness.* Tydale House Publishers Inc, 1989.

Peretti, Frank E. *This Present Darkness.* Tydale House Publishers Inc, 1986.

Piper, Don. *90 Minutes in Heaven.* Baker Publishing Group, 2004.

Smoke, Jim. *Growing Through Divorce.* Harvest House Publishers, 1955.

St. John of the Cross. *The Dark Night of the Soul.* Barnes and Noble Inc, 2005.

Thomas, Gary L. *Sacred Marriage.* Zondervan, 2000.

Thomas, Gary L. *Sacred Influence.* Zondervan, 2006.

Thomas, Gary L. *Seeking the Face of God.* Harvest House Publishers, 1994.

Tozer, A.W. *Keys to the Deeper Life.* Zondervan, 1984.

Tozer, A.W. *The Pursuit of God.* Wing Spread Publishers, 1993.

Welch, Edward T. *Depression: A Stubborn Darkness.* New Growth Press, 2004.

Whitfield MD, Charles L. *Healing the Child Within: Discovery and Recovery for Adult Children of Dysfunctional Families.* Health Communications Inc, 1987.

Yancey, Philip. *Where is God When it Hurts?* Zondervan, 1990.

Yancey, Philip. *What's So Amazing About Grace?* Zondervan, 1997.

9 781664 205390